SO-BRC-739

IMMIGRATION SERVICE
– 4 OCT 1988
DEPARTED
(1095)
HONG KONG

DEPARTMENT OF IMMIGRATION
PERMITTED TO ENTER AUSTRALIA,
on 24 APR 1986
For stay of 12 Months
SYDNEY AIRPORT 54

IMMIGRATION DIVISION BANGKOK THAILAND
A 72 DEPARTED
– 9 FEB 1987
SIGNED

IMMIGRATION ETHNIC AFFAIRS
............Person
30 OCT 1989
DEPARTED
AUSTRALIA
SYDNEY 32

THE INSIDER'S GUIDE TO
KOREA

上陸許可
ADMITTED
15. FEB. 1985
Status: 4-1- 4
Duration: 90 days
NARITA(N)
Immigration Inspector
日本国

ADMITTED
20 OCT. 1988
Status: 4-1-16
Duration 180 days
Port: HANEDA
Signature

Nº 011278

THE UNITED STATES
OF AMERICA
NONIMMIGRANT VISA
ISSUED AT
U.S. IMMIGRATION
170 HHW 1710
JUL 20 1985

PASSED
Air Port

HONG KONG
(1038)
– 7 JUN 1987
IMMIGRATION
OFFICER

THE INSIDER'S GUIDE
JAPAN • CHINA • KOREA • HAWAII • HONG KONG • AUSTRALIA
THAILAND* • BALI* • MEXICO* • INDIA*

The Insider's Guide to Korea
First Published 1987
Reprinted 1988
Hunter Publishing Inc
300 Raritan Center Parkway
CN94, Edison, N.J. 08818
by arrangement with CFW Publications Ltd

© 1988 CFW Publications Ltd

ISBN: 0 935161 69 4

Created, edited and produced by CFW Publications Ltd
130 Connaught Road C., Hong Kong
Editor in Chief: Allan Amsel
Researcher: Daniel P. Reid
Design: Hon Bing-wah/Kinggraphic
Text and artwork composed and information updated
using Xerox Ventura software

ACKNOWLEDGMENTS
The Author would like to thank Chun Shil Adams
of Seoul International Publishing House and the Korea National
Tourism Corporation for helping in various ways with the factual
information contained in this guidebook.

All rights reserved. No part of this publication may be reproduced, stored in
a retrieval system, or transmitted in any form, or by any means,
electronic, mechanical, photocopying, recording, or
otherwise, without the written permission of the publisher.

In preparation

Printed in Korea

THE INSIDER'S GUIDE TO

KOREA

by Peter Popham

Photographed by Alain Evrard

LIBRARY
COLBY-SAWYER COLLEGE
NEW LONDON, NH 03257

HUNTER PUBLISHING, INC.
Edison, N.J.

DS
982.4
.P674
1988
c.1

Contents

4

1813142l

KOREA

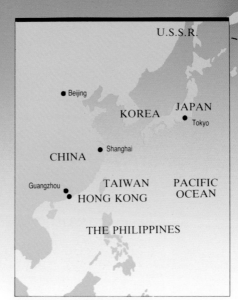

U.S.S.R.

● Beijing

KOREA   JAPAN
              ● Tokyo

CHINA   ● Shanghai

Guangzhou   TAIWAN   PACIFIC
         ●   HONG KONG   OCEAN

THE PHILIPPINES

YELLOW

● Mokp'o

● Chindo

CHEJU-DO

Cheju
●   Songsan
           ●
Halim   Hallasan
●   ●
              Sogwip'o
           ●
Taejong

N

═══ Railways
──── Roads

50km

Hongdo
●

Korea: The Hermit Emerges

KOREA TODAY

For the traveler, Korea is a country whose time has come. A flash-point of the cold war, a political embarrassment, a store-house of bitter memories, a sort of second-rate Japan without the charm – these are the negative terms in which the Republic of Korea has customarily been considered and dismissed. The reality, however, has always been much more interesting. Korea is a country with a powerful identity of its own. A

good neighbor to China, a beneficiary over the millennia of all the wealth of Chinese cultural achievement, it has never failed to interpret these gifts in its own way, infusing them with flavors found nowhere else. There is nothing in the world, for instance, like Korean food, or classical Korean pottery, or modern Korean dance. Like the Irish, to whom they are sometimes compared, centuries of oppression have done nothing to subdue these people: the crucible of hardship has fused their identity into something tough and distinctive. Even more remarkably, their troubles have failed to rob them of their humanity. Strap-hanging on the Seoul subway, the visitor is taken aback to find his heavy bag taken from him – not by a thief, but by a seated passenger, happy to relieve him of the weight for a few stops. In city

and country alike, disinterested kindness and hospitality are found everywhere. Honesty is universal.

Travelers attracted by Korea's heritage will find all manner of things to absorb them, from mountain temples to city palaces, from villages unchanged for centuries to the tombs of kings who died 1,500 or more years ago. But even for those who just want a holiday, Korea has a lot to offer: the wooded mountains of the numerous national parks, excellent beaches, the voluptuously beautiful island of Cheju-do in the south, which has almost everything and is quite unspoiled. Seoul, a crazy shambles just a year or two back when they were building the subway, is now much calmer and can be negotiated with ease. Its covered markets with their hundreds of little eateries offer an incredible banquet for the senses, even if you don't eat anything. And for high-quality clothes, shoes and bags, the city remains the bargain basement of the world.

The history of Korea is deeply sad, a bitter saga of wars and invasions, and the worst is not over yet. The slicing of the country into two hostile states, still effectively at war with each other more than thirty years after the end of hostilities, is a situation no Korean can resign himself to happily. But with economic success, and the international recognition symbolized by the decision to stage the 1988 Olympics in the country, the Republic is riding a wave of self-confidence, and part of that is seen in the welcome they offer visitors. First-class hotels are abundant in Seoul, Kyongju, Pusan, and Cheju-do, while simpler accommodation is obtainable at every fork in the road. New expressways augment the punctual and comfortable trains and the dense network of fast and frequent (though somewhat

ABOVE Traditional houses in Seoul's Pangsang-dong section, tightly nested together and RIGHT a more spacious feeling created in the striking architecture of Kyobo Building in the city's Chongjin-dong district.

10

hair-raising) buses: a self-propelled vacation in Korea is now a real possibility, and will become an even more useful one when rent-a-car facilities are expanded. The Korea National Tourism Corporation has an elaborate information office in the center of Seoul, and an impressive array of well-produced literature in English. People continue to assert that *han'gul*, the Korean writing system, is one of the world's easiest alphabets (and it's true that it's not difficult), but the realization that most visitors to the Olympics are unlikely to go to the trouble of learning it is slowly sinking in, and more and more restaurants are investing in romanized menus.

Once known as the Hermit Kingdom on account of its introspective ways, Korea has emerged into the strong light of international curiosity, and it's looking good: compact, cheap, easily traveled, lots of fun. Its women are beautiful. It's a sheer holiday, and an education in history, culture and human resilience, rolled into one.

"THE COUNTRY THAT STANDS ON END"

Roughly forty million people live in the Republic of Korea which, with an area of 99,000 sq km (38,224 sq miles), is smaller than the communist north, 122,000 sq km (47,104 sq miles). The peninsula as a whole is comparable in size to Great Britain or New York State. Located between 43 degrees and 34 degrees north, it stretches 1,000 km (620 miles) from north to south and 216 km (134 miles) from east to west at its narrowest point. To the west lie the Yellow Sea and China, to the east the East Sea (Sea of Japan) and the southwest extreme of the Japanese archipelago. Scattered along the rugged coastline are over three thousand islands.

Korea is a land of mountains, and wherever you are, even in central Seoul, the skyline is bounded by low but craggy peaks, ridge upon ridge of them. So ubiquitous are they that Korea has been nicknamed "the country that stands on end." The spaces in between devoted to agriculture and industry, well watered by the short, twisting, fast-flowing rivers, constitute just twenty per cent of the total area.

Though it's hard to appreciate the fact while traveling through the country, the whole peninsula is on a tilt, the highest peaks being in the east of the country and sloping erratically to lower

land in the west. On the east coast the magnificent Diamond Mountains drop precipitously to the sea, where fishing coves alternate with sandy beaches. The west coast is riddled with shallow, narrow inlets where tidal changes, amounting in some places to twenty-five feet, are among the most extreme in the world. The many islands off this coast are the peaks of long-submerged mountains.

Though ravaged by the civil war, the Korean countryside is once again rich in colorful flora and exotic fauna. The mountains, many of them stripped almost bare of vegetation at one time (some blame the greedy Japanese colonizers, others say they were decimated by the demand for fuel for the *ondol* under-floor heating systems), have been intensively reforested with trees native to the peninsula such as pine and juniper, maple and cherry. Nowadays it would take a very keen eye to spot signs of past

damage.

Much effort has also been thrown into conserving the country's wildlife, and today you'll see egrets and herons feeding in the paddies, pheasants and magpies in the bushes, kingfishers, woodpeckers and hoopoes perching in the trees. In one of the weirdest of the many ironies of the civil war's aftermath, the no-man's-land along the 38th parallel,

the so-called Demilitarized Zone (DMZ), uncultivated for 30 years and more, has become quite accidentally a nature reserve where among other endangered species the splendid Manchurian crane, a symbol of longevity throughout the East with its snow-white plumage, red feather cap and black-trimmed wings, takes refuge from the folly of mankind.

CLIMATE

Korea has a temperate continental climate with four distinct seasons. It is affected by both the bitter cold fronts which reach down from Siberia in the north, and the annual monsoon rains of the Pacific region to the south, which drench the country in late June and July. Winters are cold and dry, though the whole country also receives a fair amount of snow, even Cheju-do Island far to the south, which is so mild for most of the year that it does without *ondol*. Winters in the Republic are naturally less severe than in the north, though only Eskimos would deliberately choose to visit in this season. Summers by contrast are hot and humid everywhere, with temperatures rising to 37°C (98°F).

Unquestionably the best seasons to visit the country are spring and autumn, when the days are warm and balmy, the nights crisp and cool, and the countryside, whether bright with blossoms or fiery with autumn leaves, looks its best and most ravishing.

A TURBULENT HISTORY

THE FIRST THREE THOUSAND YEARS

The ancestors of the present-day Korean people were migrant tribes, cul-

The lively ceiling decoration CENTER at the Toksu Palace, Seoul which probably dates back to the sixteenth century, depicts the dragon motif symbolizing authority and longevity.

ally and linguistically connected with the Finns, Mongols and Turks, who streamed down into the peninsula from northern and central Asia some 30,000 years ago. They constituted the most easterly outpost of Altaic culture. Thousands of years of interaction with the Japanese, whom they closely resemble physically, and the Chinese, to whom they are indebted for much of their culture, have complicated matters, but both in culture and language Korea remains a distinct and homogeneous entity. Take the language, for example. Along with the writing system, Korea borrowed a vast vocabulary from the Chinese, which remains the backbone of the nation's learning - yet the way of pronouncing these borrowed words is distinctly their own. Korean shares an identical sentence structure with Japanese, evidence of closely intertwined roots, yet the differences, too, are deep.

The Korean creation myth is curious and instructive. Hwanung, son of the divine creator, descended from heaven and proclaimed himself king of all he surveyed. While he was looking over his domain, he overheard the fervent prayers of a bear that desired to become human. Taking pity on the beast, Hwanung gave it twenty pieces of garlic and some mugwort, and told it to retire to a cave for a hundred days. The bear did as it was told. When it emerged, it was the first human woman.

This woman prayed for a son, became pregnant through divine favor, and shortly gave birth to one Tan-gun, who in 2333 BC became the first human king and the founder of Korea. His reign was of the epic length favored in those days - more than 1,200 years in fact, ending in 1122 BC. Tan-gun or National Foundation Day is still cele-

brated every year on October 3. (Most of Korea's public holidays are concentrated in the fall, by common consent the most agreeable season.)

The creation myth is interesting on account of the venerable age it accords to the nation's still quite striking attachment to garlic. It also suggests that herbal medicine goes back a long way into the nation's prehistory: mugwort remains an important ingredient in traditional cures.

At the end of Tan-gun's reign, the myth continues (now transmuting qui-

RIGHT Korea's largest standing stone Buddha, the Unjin Miruk at Nonsan, glimpsed through the windows of Kwanchok-sa Temple.

etly into legend), the primordial China connection was made: one King Kija arrived in the peninsula, a direct descendant of the Chinese Shang dynasty which collapsed that same year. 1122 BC thus saw the establishment of new dynasties in both China and Korea, and though the date is merely traditional, the story does attest to the ancient and largely fraternal links between Korea and its giant neighbor. China was the Central Kingdom, Korea was "Choson," the Land of Morning Calm. Korean kings, like Chinese emperors, took the dragon as their symbol of divine authority, but whereas the Chinese dragon had five claws, the Korean had only four - just to discourage people from entertaining foolish ideas.

The steady development of civilization in the peninsula during the first three millennia BC is evident in the wealth of archaeological remains. One of the oldest is the possibly Paleolithic dolmen still standing on the island of Kanghwa, near Seoul, which may date from the twentieth century BC. Sophisticated pottery remains from the first

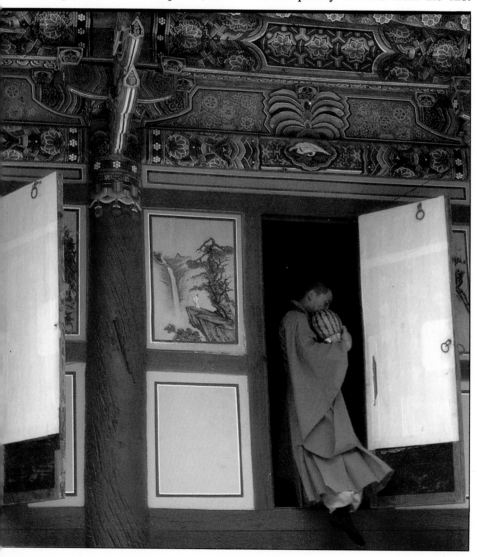

millennia BC are not uncommon, then the elaborate articles produced by a Bronze Age culture which came down from Siberia via Manchuria begin to appear. This culture stimulated the appearance of tribal leagues, replacing the smaller clan organizations of the stone age, but was rapidly supplanted by iron-wielding groups which came down from northern China.

The first historically proven Chinese invasion of the peninsula came in 108 BC. After the Han Dynasty had put an end to dissent within China, the Han emperor Wu-ti invaded the ancient kingdom of Chosun and the regime he established retained control of the country for more than 400 years. Then in 313 AD the Koguryo tribe, based in the north of the country, which had been steadily growing in power for centuries, took advantage of the disintegration to wrest control of northern Korea and southeastern Manchuria from the Chinese. Though it adopted China's advanced military and administrative systems, Koguryo remained ethnically and culturally Korean.

THREE KINGDOMS: A CHINESE MIRROR

Meanwhile, further south on the Korean peninsula, two other powerful tribes emerged: the Paekche, which carved a kingdom out of the south-west corner, and the Shilla, which dominated the entire eastern portion of the peninsula. Like the three kingdoms who supplanted the Han dynasty in China, these three Korean kingdoms engaged in constant internecine warfare and political intrigue, and their relationship was marked by rapidly shifting alliances. Like the Three Kingdoms period in China, this was also in Korea an

era of great turbulence and intellectual ferment.

In 618, the house of T'ang defeated all other rivals for the Dragon Throne, and reunited the Chinese empire for the first time since the fall of Han. One of the T'ang dynasty's first objectives was to establish effective control over the Korean peninsula. In 645 and again in 647, T'ang armies attacked the Koguryo kingdom but failed to conquer it. So adopting the time-honored Chinese strategy of "using barbarians to subdue barbarians," the T'ang court formed an alliance with the southern Shilla kingdom, and together they defeated Paekche in 660 and 667. T'ang China next tried to vanquish Shilla as well.

Shilla, however, rebelled against T'ang hegemony, giving aid and encouragement to insurgents in Paekche and Koguryo, too. Under the Shilla banner the three men later eulogized as the unifiers of the nation, King Muyol, his successor King Munmu, and their military commander, General Kim, fought against heavy odds to drive the Chinese back across the Taedong River, north of the present North Korean capi-

ABOVE RIGHT Buddhist painting at Pomo-sa Temple near Pusan, headquarters of the Dyana sect.

16

tal, P'yongyang, and unify the entire Korean peninsula. In the process, Shilla also succeeded in establishing dominion over Paekche and Koguryo. An agreement was then drawn up which saved China's face on the one hand, and ensured Shilla's future security and independence on the other. According to this, Shilla would remain an independent Korean kingdom, but would also become an official tributary state of China, and acknowledge China's supremacy in the region. The art of diplomatic hair-splitting is by no means a new one.

THE PENINSULA UNITED

Historians generally agree that this unification of the peninsula in the seventh century by Shilla is the beginning of Korea's history as a united nation. Though this unity sometimes proved chimerical in subsequent centuries, it persisted more or less intact until the partitioning of the country in 1945.

The flow of Chinese cultural institutions into the peninsula, which had got seriously under way during the Three Kingdoms Period, continued after the

triumph of Shilla. The Confucian principles of organizing society, which had evolved in China during the Han era, were gradually adopted in Korea as well, though with modifications. In particular the Korean ruling-class was unable to overcome its distaste for the egalitarianism intrinsic to the Chinese bureaucracy, whereby candidates of any and all social ranks could compete for positions in government. As in Japan, the form of the civil service examination was adopted, but in reality high office was reserved for the children of the aristocracy.

Under Chinese influence, the Three Kingdoms and Shilla Periods also saw the establishment of Buddhism throughout the peninsula, and a terrific flourishing of the associated arts and crafts, as well as the Chinese writing system.

During the United Shilla Dynasty that followed Shilla's military defeat of the Chinese, Korea began to exert strong influence on Japan, at this time emerging from the primitive twilight. As the closest point on the Asian continent to the Japanese archipelago, Korea was the route through which Chinese culture traveled to Japan, picking up a distinctive Korean flavor on the way. Korean scholars became tutors to the Japanese imperial house, and so many others traveled to Japan to serve in the administration that a family register made in 815 reveals that fully one-third of Japan's noble families were of Korean descent. This fact is ironic in the light of Japan's attempt earlier this century to stigmatize the Koreans as barbaric and to extinguish their language and culture in favor of Japan's.

As the T'ang dynasty in China began to crumble during the ninth century, so did the Shilla. Various branches of the royal clan plotted to seize power, peasants revolted and bandits ran amok

---

Musicians in annual Confucian ceremony at Chongmyo shrine, Seoul. The instrument is called a Pyonggyong; the chimes are made of a jade-like stone.

through the country. The Shilla dynasty began to fragment as petty kings set up petty tyrannies within its frontiers.

Then, just about the time that the house of Sung re-unified China, the Korean house of Koryo succeeded in doing the same thing for the peninsula. The dynasty they founded in 918 was to last for 450 years.

KORYO: A CULTURAL PEAK

The Koryo dynasty, from which the word Korea derives, was founded, not by an aristocrat but by the son of a merchant, Wang Kon by name. He was also the first ruler of the peninsula to invoke the Chinese concept of the "mandate of heaven," meaning that his claim to the throne was based on moral rather than hereditary grounds.

The dominant cultural role during the Koryo dynasty was played by Buddhism, which was generously patronized by the Koryo kings and became a powerful force in politics. Numerous temples and pagodas were built, and Buddhist statuary attained new peaks of artistic excellence. In fact, the early years of Koryo were a flourishing time for Korean culture in general. Celadon porcelain was mastered by the nation's potters, who went on to make works unsurpassed even by the Chinese. The principle of movable type was invented by a Korean, and books were printed with it, two hundred years before Gutenberg started doing the same thing in Europe. Intellectually the most important event was the introduction from China of the ideas of Neo-Confucianism, which brought about the first organized intellectual opposition to Buddhism.

Like the Sung dynasty in China, Koryo was plagued by political pressures from the north. The northern Khitan tribe, after sacking the Sung capital and sending the court into exile, attempted in 993 to invade Koryo, but was successfully repelled. The next

challenge, however, demolished everything in its path: the Mongol alliance, led by Genghis Khan, which destroyed all rivals on the northern steppes and then began its relentless campaign to conquer China and the rest of the known world.

In 1231 Ghengis Khan's troops attacked Korea in full force, but met with unexpectedly stiff resistance. Meanwhile the Koryo court retreated into exile on Kanghwa Island (taking advantage of the Mongols' one weakness, fear of the sea), and there the king ordered the engraving on 80,000 wooden tablets of the *Tripitaka Koreana*, based on the complete Chinese translation of the Buddhist Scripture. Once it was completed the entire work was committed to the flames - an offering to the gods to enlist their protection against the Mongols. (Another complete set of the Scriptures was later carved, and is preserved at the famous Haein Temple, near Taegu. (See **Korea: The Broad Highway**, page 73)

LIVING WITH THE MONGOLS

Their prayers were only partially answered. When the Mongols set up their Yuan dynasty in China, Koryo was

Embroidered decoration on the costume of officiating Confucian priest at Chongmyo shrine, central Seoul. OPPOSITE Archaic front view of Confucian scholar at Chongmyo.

18

obliged to come to terms with them. The country was allowed a show of independence and continued to rule most of the peninsula, but in reality it was a tributary state of the Yuan. And the Koryo was forced to accept many distasteful conditions: the crown princes were obliged to go to the new Chinese capital, Peking, for their education, to marry Mongol princesses, and to remain there as hostages until the reigning Koryo king died. By this means the Mongols gained effective control of the country, without having to go to the trouble of conquering it. They also extorted a heavy annual tribute in the form of gold, silver, ginseng and women.

When Chinese rebels under the leadership of the peasant general Chu Yuan-chang routed the Mongols and drove them back across the Great Wall, Korea gained a brief reprieve. The hundred-year-long humiliation was over. But within twenty years of the establishment of the Ming dynasty in 1386, the Chinese were once again trying to gain control of Korea. An invading army was dispatched to the country, and the Koryo court responded by sending a fiery young commander named Yi Song-gye to repel the invaders.

Yi realized, however, that his army stood no chance of success against the superior Ming force, so he turned back and promptly deposed the Koryo king, at first replacing him with the crown prince but later taking the throne himself. In 1392, invoking the mandate of heaven, Yi established the Yi dynasty, also known as the Choson dynasty, Choson being the ancient Chinese name for Korea. It was to become both Korea's last and its longest dynasty, surviving until the Japanese annexation in 1910. Yi, who was given the title T'aejo or Founding Father of the new dynasty, immediately re-established traditional tributary relations with China, adopted Neo-Confucianism as the

new state creed, and re-named his kingdom Choson, in the Chinese style. He moved the capital of the nation to Hanyang, the city known today as Seoul.

YI: THE LONGEST ERA

The adoption of Neo-Confucianism, which had first reared its head during the Koryo period, was highly significant for Korean society. For one thing, it mollified the conservative Ming court, which commenced to regard Korea once again as a dutiful younger brother, capable of managing its own affairs. For another, it greatly reduced the influence of Buddhism, both at court and in the daily life of the people. Confucian burial rites, for instance, took the place of Buddhist cremation, and ancestor-worship and other Confucian practices became de rigueur.

King Sejong, the fourth Yi ruler, who reigned from 1418 to 1450, is gen-

Though the Japanese triumphed easily on land, at sea it was a different matter. The commander of the Korean fleet, Admiral Yi Sun-shin gave his navy an unexpected advantage with his invention of the world's first armor-plated warships, called Turtle Ships on account of their humped appearance. Propelled by oars and heavily armed with cannon, these compact, highly-maneuverable vessels had decks and gunwales plated with spike-studded sheets of heavy iron, making them impossible to board and practically invulnerable to enemy projectiles. Though greatly outnumbered by the Japanese, Admiral Yi's handful of Turtle Ships sent the Japanese into a panic, sinking more than 250 ships in the course of eight battles and forcing the Japanese to withdraw before they had succeeded even in setting foot on Chinese soil.

Provoked by Korea's stubborn resistance, Hideyoshi launched another attack in 1597. Admiral Yi, meanwhile, had fallen victim to Korean court intrigues and had lost his post. His successor sallied forth to meet the second Japanese onslaught - and promptly lost all but a dozen of the Korean fleet. Yi was hastily recalled, and with only this handful of ships at his disposal once again routed the numerically superior Japanese, sinking or capturing most of their ships and putting the rest to flight. During the final battle of the war, Yi was struck by a stray bullet and killed. He continues to live on in the popular imagination as Korea's greatest military leader, and his armored statue still glares down from its pedestal in central Seoul.

erally regarded as Korea's greatest king. He filled the highest offices with men of merit, and under his influence the nation's culture flourished as never before. It was King Sejong who personally supervised the creation of *han'gul*, the unique Korean alphabet which freed Korean literature and education from its cumbersome dependence on complex ideograms.

Once again, however, the nation's hard-earned calm was soon rudely shattered by outside events. This time the intrusion came from Japan, when the shogun Hideyoshi launched his megalomanic campaign to conquer China in 1592. The Yi court declined to participate, and in retribution Hideyoshi attacked Korea with a force of 150,000 men. The Japanese army swept through the peninsula, overwhelming Korea's land defenses in less than a month and wreaking such havoc wherever they went that the Koreans have never forgotten nor forgiven it.

ABOVE Relic of Shilla dynasty Buddhist image in stone, preserved at the National Museum, Kyongju.

Hideyoshi's death in 1598 persuaded the Japanese to abandon their continental adventure, but the ensuing peace was once again short-lived. The Manchus came next, when their leader Nurhachi initiated his own campaign to conquer Ming China. In 1627, Manchu cavalry swept down from the north and captured both P'yongyang and Seoul, forcing the Yi court to break off its long-standing tributary relationship with China and become a Manchu vassal instead.

In 1636, Korea rebelled against the Manchu overlords, and in response the Manchus once again crossed the Yalu River in force, this time capturing the entire court and exacting heavy revenge. Eight years later, in 1644, they decisively defeated the Ming in China, occupied Peking, and established China's last dynasty, the Ching. Korea became a tributary state of Ching, and remained so until Japan wrested control away from China at the turn of the present century. Interestingly, the last dynasties of both China and Korea were to fall within a year of each other.

LICKING THE WOUNDS

After the consecutive traumas of the Japanese and Manchu invasions, which left the whole country in ruins and the people instilled with a fear of all foreigners, Korea pulled back into its shell and enforced a policy of thoroughgoing isolation. It became the Hermit Kingdom, insular and aloof - and, in consequence, lamentably ill-equipped to meet the challenges of a new age when, in the nineteenth century, the European and Japanese imperialists came knocking loudly on the door. Korea strove manfully to keep them all out, but with the Ching dynasty in Peking, its ostensible protector, in a state of terminal decline, collapse was only a matter of time.

From the middle of the nineteenth century the Hermit Kingdom had been proving less than hermetic, and Western learning had begun to filter into the country by way of Peking. Much of this came via Catholic missionaries, who naturally tried to spread their faith at the same time. The Yi court, however, regarded Catholicism as a serious threat to Korea's traditional Confucian order and tried to suppress it. The court issued repeated warnings and edicts against the Christian faith and severely punished offenders. In 1866, nine French Catholic priests were publicly executed on the banks of the Han River in Seoul, and 8,000 Korean converts were massacred in the pogroms that followed.

The Chinese were the only foreigners freely admitted into Korea during these years. European and American diplomats and merchants were excluded rigorously, and this policy was extended to include the Japanese when it was felt that they had been tainted by Western influence. The Japanese took offense at this, and in 1875 deliberately provoked an incident between ships of their navy and Korean coastal defenses. Taking its cue from Western "gunboat diplomacy," Japan used the ensuing peace negotiations to force Korea to permit Japanese diplomatic and trade missions to be established on Korean soil.

Japanese influence on the peninsula grew rapidly in the wake of that treaty, much to the dismay of the Korean government, which was still nominally a tributary of China. Chinese troops were sent from Peking to re-assert Ching authority, and clashed repeatedly on Korean soil with Japanese forces.

Years of aggressive foreign pressure, Japanese, Chinese and Western, provoked a patriotic and xenophobic reaction which found expression in the

RIGHT The Un Dang *Yogwan* in Seoul, formally the house of a nobleman, and one of the few which offer a rich experience of the traditional way of Korean life.

Tonghak ("Eastern Learning") Movement, a grassroots social and religious movement which proposed applying traditional Eastern learning to the task of keeping out the foreigners and saving the country from ruin. These efforts culminated in the Tonghak Uprising of 1894, which in turn sparked off the Sino-Japanese War. A small peasant uprising in Cholla Province led quickly to major rebel victories over government forces, causing the government to petition China for assistance. China sent an army across the Yalu to help the Korean government to suppress the revolt, at which Japan responded by sending an army of its own into the peninsula.

JAPAN'S LITTLE EMPIRE

Within a year Japan had dealt the decadent Ching court a comprehensive and humiliating defeat, and forced it to accept the terms of the Treaty of Shimonoseki, which formally ended hostilities on April 17, 1895. This treaty guaranteed Korea's independence from China - a doubtful blessing, for in China's place the treaty gave Japan a key role in Korean affairs, a role which led to outright annexation fifteen years later. Japan also demanded and got control of both the Ryukyu Islands (Okinawa) and Taiwan, and formally annexed both the same year.

The next uninvited guest at the banquet Korea was haplessly making of itself for the modernized nations was Russia, which competed fiercely with Japan for influence at the Korean court. The eventual consequence of this was the Russo-Japanese War of 1904, when the Japanese once again showed the mettle of their new armed forces by obtaining a clear victory. In the aftermath Japan immediately occupied Korea, and in the Treaty of Portsmouth, which ended hostilities on September 5, 1905, Japan's control over Korea was given international recognition. It was a small step from this to the rendering of Korea into Japan's very own Western-style colony. Japan's resident-general became the ultimate authority in Korea, wielding total control over the country's foreign relations, internal administration and police force.

Korean patriots offered stiff resistance to the Japanese, and formed guerrilla bands to harass them. In 1909 the Japanese resident-general, Ito Hirobumi, was assassinated by a Korean patriot while visiting Harbin in Manchuria, and in retaliation Japan dictated a new treaty the following year, under which Korea was annexed entirely and Korean statehood abolished.

From then on, the Japanese ruled Korea with an iron fist, ruthlessly suppressing any sign of opposition. The greatest threat to their authority came in 1919 when Korean nationalists, in common with other victims of colonialism in many other nations, submitted a petition to the Versailles Conference demanding independence. When their demand was rejected they unilaterally published a "declaration of independence,ence" demanding the immediate withdrawal of Japanese forces. As the movement gathered momentum, and peeaceful demonstrations began to occur spontaneously throughout the country, the Japanese police panicked, and attacked the patriots week after week with brutally excessive force,

leaving thousands of unarmed civilians dead. The few concessions they subsequently made to Korean pride did nothing to weaken their grip on the country, but in the longer perspective the independence movement had some positive consequences for Korea. It gave the lie to the Japanese myth that their control of Korea was benign and had the support of the mass of the people; and it did much to develop a sense of national solidarity among Koreans.

KOREA'S DARK VALLEY

As the militarists in the Japanese government gained the upper hand during the 1930s, repression in Korea once again increased, and a cruel campaign was launched to eradicate Korean culture and replace it with Japanese models. Ancient palaces and temples were razed or bulldozed, masters of Korean arts were killed or interned to prevent

OPPOSITE PAGE Baggy traditional garments and wonderful hats are still often seen in rural areas of Korea; but ABOVE city children are as gaudy and individualistic in their choice of clothes as Americans.

With the defeat of the Japanese in 1945, Korea enjoyed yet another of its pathetically brief interludes of peace. Two new occupying forces now swarmed across the country, the Russian and the American, disarming the Japanese, and while the arbitrarily selected 38th Parallel was initially intended merely as a demarcation line for the efforts of these allied forces, it soon hardened into an unbreachable boundary between powers which proved to have very different plans for Korea's future. The Russians went straight to work establishing a fully-fledged Communist regime in the north, with Kim Il-sung as its ruler, while the Americans withdrew from the south, which quickly fell into political disarray.

In September 1947, the United Nations called for the establishment of a united and independent Korean state, and suggested that national elections be held to determine its government. The Soviet Union, however, refused to permit the UN to supervise elections in the north, and so they were held only in the south. On August 15, 1948 the Republic of Korea came officially into being, with Syngman Rhee as its democratically elected (and very right-wing) president and Seoul as its capital. The Soviet-controlled north reacted by establishing the Democratic Republic of Korea on September 9 of the same year, with Kim Il-sung as head of state and P'yongyang as its capital. For the first time since the uniting of the Three Kingdoms under the Shilla dynasty in the seventh century, Korea found itself divided into politically antagonistic entities.

them from spreading Korean culture to a new generation. Korean history was summarily dropped from school curricula, and all courses were subsequently taught entirely in Japanese. Koreans were forced to adopt Japanese names, the Japanese language and Japanese manners. Thousands of Korean men were pressed into Japan's armed forces or shipped to Japan as slave labor for the war effort, while Korean women were rounded up to perform as prostitutes for Japan's occupation troops.

Japanese colonial rule in Korea brought significant material improvements in terms of new schools, hospitals, roads, railways and communication systems, and stimulated the modernization of industry and agriculture. But as in colonies everywhere, the country's development was oriented to the needs of the colonial power, and the country's labor and resources were relentlessly exploited for the benefit of Japan. Awareness of the richness of Korea's national heritage has been slow to reawaken; bitterness at the rapacity of Japanese power has been equally slow to dissipate.

By the end of 1948, Russian and American troops had withdrawn from their opposite ends of the peninsula, but

ABOVE Setting sun over Seoul. RIGHT In Seoul's Namsan Park, forsythia and cherry blossoms leave city dwellers in no doubt that spring has sprung.

while the United States did little to enhance the south's defenses, the Russians continued to pour arms and advisers into the north, building up a formidable North Korean army. Then in January 1950, the American Secretary of State declared in public that Korea lay beyond the pale of America's vital interests. The North Koreans, confident of their superiority in arms, were not slow to take the hint and on June 25, 1950 launched a full-scale invasion of the south.

With the Soviet delegate to the United Nations conveniently not in attendance, the United States managed to get a UN resolution passed branding the North Koreans as aggressors, and pledging UN troops in the south's defense. Although the great majority of the troops sent to resist the north were American, the forces of 15 other nations fought North Korea under the United Nations flag.

At first the invaders from the north routed the UN troops, and nearly succeeded in driving them clean off the peninsula: the southern port city of Pusan was the only center of population they did not reach. But then General Douglas MacArthur, the American commander, conceived and executed a daring amphibious landing at Inch'on, west of Seoul, cutting off over-extended North Korean forces and turning the tide of the war. Despite strong warnings from China not to do so, MacArthur pursued the enemy across the 38th Parallel deep into the north.

As United States forces approached the Manchurian border, Chinese troops suddenly began pouring across the Yalu River, drove the UN side back across the 38th Parallel again and recaptured Seoul. For the first time in history Chinese and American soldiers confronted each other on the battlefield, but for Korea the scene was all-too familiar. "When whales fight, the shrimp gets hurt;" says a Korean proverb, and the Korean War hurt the country more than any previous conflict. Bloody battles raged back and forth across the peninsula, with heavy casualtiies and massive destruction on both sides.

EYEBALL TO EYEBALL

Finally, on July 27, 1953, an armistice ended the fighting and formally divided Korea at the 38th Parallel, with a three-mile wide Demilitarized Zone (DMZ) in between. This belt of no-man's-land is supervised by a joint north/south Military Armistice Commission, which has been meeting regularly at P'anmunjom since 1953 to discuss alleged truce violations and exchange accusations. They are the longest continuing truce talks in the history of human cussedness.

At the end of the Korean War, Syngman Rhee presided over a nation laid waste by modern warfare and a government staffed entirely by his personal protégés. Seoul and most of the countryside were in ruins, industry and agriculture had ground to a halt, and corruption was rampant at every level of government. As conditions grew steadily worse during the 1950s, popular resentment against the Rhee regime began to gather momentum.

Elections were held again in 1960, but they were so obviously rigged in Rhee's favor that anti-government demonstrations flared up all over the country. The culminating event came in Seoul, when police fired on angry crowds and killed 115 people. Under heavy pressure from all sides, Rhee wisely resigned from office and retired to Hawaii, where he died in 1965.

On August 15, 1960 South Korea's Second Republic was established under the leadership of Rhee's former opponents in the Democratic Party. The new

RIGHT United Nations soldier standing guard at P'anmunjom, the only place where the Koreas meet. The height and other dimensions of the two flags have been the subject of endless exercises in one-upmanship.

government was refreshingly open and liberal, but soon proved to be hopelessly ineffectual in dealing with the country's pressing problems, and was toppled by a military coup in May 1961. A military dictatorship with a strong anti-Communist stance took over, and before long Major-General Park Chung Hee emerged as its leader. Park called for new elections in 1963, retired from the military, and ran successfully for president. He was inaugurated in December, and Korea's Third Republic was launched.

IN PARK'S POCKET

Park won a second presidential term in 1967, and then in 1969 he forced through a constitutional amendment which permitted him to run yet again. In 1971 he narrowly defeated opposition leader Kim Dae-jung for a third presidential term, and the following year tightened his stranglehold on Korean affairs by declaring martial law. He took all effective political power into his own hands, and ruled by decree.

Despite the arbitrary nature of his regime, Korea did attain a degree of stability under Park, and the economy took great strides. His government threw its full support behind industrial growth, with special emphasis on exports, and during the 1960s the economy achieved a spectacular annual growth rate of over 40 percent. Even during the 1970s, as other countries struggled to cope with the oil crisis, Korea maintained a steady export growth of about 15 percent per year. By 1979 the total value of Korea's exports had topped US$14 billion.

The nation's economic development was well-planned from the outset. Heavy industries were distributed through the country, not concentrated in and around the capital. Modern expressways were built which gave rapid access to the new centers of industry both from Seoul and from the international seaports of Pusan and Inch'on.

Initially the great bulk of assistance went to heavy industry, but a serious attempt was made to right this with the creation in 1970 of the Saemaul (New Community) Movement, which aimed to modernize agriculture and rural life in general through spurring villagers to help themselves. The results are seen everywhere one travels in the countryside: neat villages of modern brick houses, usually with a metal church spire somewhere in their midst; neatly-tilled fields, blinding with vinyl sleeves; and innumerable small tractors and harvesters at work (though you will also be delighted to spot the occasional farmer plowing his patch with the help of an ox, or trundling into market behind a bullock).

The Park era came abruptly to an end on October 26, 1979, when the president was assassinated at a banquet by the hand-picked chief of his own security organization, the Korean CIA. The assassin claimed that his motive was simply to end Park's dictatorial hold over the country and restore democracy, but the court gave him little sympathy, and he and six accomplices were convicted and executed. After 18 years under Park's rule, the Republic of Korea suddenly found itself in a frightening political vacuuum.

The answer, after a brief hiatus when Park's prime minister held the reins, was another strong man from the army. In August 1980 General Chun Doo Hwan took charge, and the next month was formally inaugurated as president. He remains in charge today, though he is pledged to relinquish control by 1988, when presidential elections are due to be held.

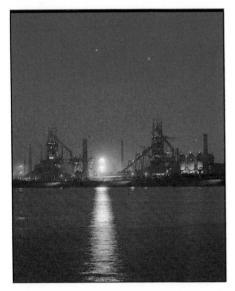

PROSPERITY AND PROTEST

Under Chun, the nation's economy has continued to prosper but steps toward democracy have so far been tentative at best. Kim Dae-jung, President Park's old *bête noir,* returned from exile in the United States, but both he and the other most prominent opposition politician, Kim Young-sam, found their potential for action closely restricted by Chun. Eager to present the world with a clean, respectable, democratic face, yet lacking a popular base of his own and terrified of the advantage North Korea might take of any sign of weakness,

Chun walks a difficult path.

Despite the fantastic economic achievements, which have put the Republic in a different league from the north and have done much to narrow the gap between rich and poor and city- and country-dwellers, its way forward is by no means clear. Democracy is keenly desired, as the passionate anti-Chun demonstrations on Seoul's campuses each spring make clear. But the nation's experience of democracy is almost nil, and attempts in the near-future to make it work will doubtless have to put up

with having the military hovering nervously in the background, ready to intervene at any moment. When the basic question of how the country should be governed is fraught with such difficulties, it is not surprising that the larger issue of how the peninsula might be united is even tougher to resolve. But that improbable event is surely the desideratum at the back of most Koreans' minds. Until it comes to pass, even massive prosperity will not succeed in cloaking the fact that, on either side of the DMZ, what is being lived is only half a life.

Symbols, OPPOSITE, of State and ABOVE of growing industrial sophistication.

31

The
Culture
of
Korea

LIBRARY
COLBY-SAWYER COLLEGE
NEW LONDON, NH 03257

A STUBBORN STRAIN

A trait of epic stubbornness has enabled Korea to hang on to the particulars of its culture through thick and thin; the little hiccup which goes by the name of modernization has so far failed miserably to turn the country into a clone of New Jersey, Birmingham or Osaka, however much it may in superficial ways have come to resemble them. Growing prosperity has indeed in one sense had the opposite effect: it has permitted evidence of the wealth of their tradition, many Koreans who lived through the period of Japanese domination experience deep emotion. Gazing at the amazingly beautiful and serene stone Buddha in Sokkuram grotto, near Kyongju, one guide remarked, "Every time I come here I feel I've found something that we lost a long, long time ago."

For the visitor, Korea's rich mix of cultural elements, most of which are in varying degrees unfamiliar, can be baffling. In the space of a few weeks' stay in Seoul he might witness ancient rites

money and effort to go into rediscovering or even re-creating what has been lost. Potters now travel to Japan to study the techniques that disappeared from the peninsula when Hideyoshi's invaders prevailed on the country's best artisans to go back to Japan with them. Immense care is taken to preserve and display the archaeological relics dug up in places like Kyongju, capital during the Shilla period, and to restore extant historical sites to their original condition. Confronted by this of Confucianism, Buddhism and Shamanism, as well as attending a crowded Catholic mass and a superb recital of classical European music. He is entitled to know how it all fits together, and what sort of sense it makes.

RELIGION

SHAMAN ROOTS

When disaster befalls a Korean household – if one of the members falls seriously ill, or if the house is repeatedly burgled, or if the husband seems bent on tearing the family apart by spending all his money on his mistress – a traditional Korean housewife knows that there is only one thing to be done: call in a reputable *mudang* and conduct a *kut*.

The *mudang* is a shamanistic medium, and the *kut* is the elaborate ceremony, lasting long hours and sometimes all night, through which, to the accompaniment of cacophonous music, the *mudang* communicates with the spirits infesting the house, driving out the evil ones and placating the benevolent ones with offerings of food, drink and money. The closest analogy in the West is the exorcism rite, and as in an exorcism the *mudang*'s role involves her being taken over by several spirits in turn while she is in a trance. Her behavior in this state may be wild and unpredictable, and invariably leaves her exhausted.

Belief in the spirit world and in the

necessity of interceding with it is found all over the world, from Haiti to the suburbs of south-east England, but perhaps nowhere else has it retained so strong a hold on the popular imagination over such a long period of time.

Shamanism is the basic bedrock of Korean culture. The word *shaman,* which entered English through German, is Siberian in origin, and the tissue of beliefs and practices with which it is associated probably entered the peninsula with the Altaic settlers from the north, deep in the prehistoric past. Quite early it made the jump to Japan, where it slowly mutated into what is known as the "indigenous" religion, Shinto.

Like Shinto, Korean shamanism benefited from the tolerant attitude of Buddhism, which had become the state religion of the whole peninsula by the sixth century, Shilla being the last kingdom to succumb to it. Suppression of practices inimical to Buddhism, such as human sacrifice, occurred gradually during the following centuries, but there was no systematic attempt to outlaw shamanism. It has retained a great deal of popular loyalty right up to the present.

Confucianism, more a civil code than a religion, was unsympathetic to shamanism but failed to uproot it. In fact, according to one theory, it unintentionally gave shamanism an extra lease of life. In the pre-Confucian days, *mudang* came in both sexes. When the male-chauvinistic code of Confucianism became established, Korean women found themselves at the bottom of the heap. Not only had they lost hope of attaining high status in society, but even the basic human pleasures, sexual pleasure included, were denied them and regarded as insignificant. The result, it is suggested, was a terrific incidence of

OPPOSITE Some of the thousands of woodblocks inscribed with Buddhist texts which have resided for more than 700 years at the Haein-sa Temple. LEFT Gilt statue of a Bodhisattva from the United Shilla Kingdom (668-935).

sexual frustration, manifested in what today would be regarded as nervous breakdowns, but were in those days interpreted as signs that the women concerned had become vessels of the spirit world. Such women became *mudang*, thereby regaining social status of a sort, and obtaining the ecstatic release their husbands denied them at the same time.

All *mudang* today, apparently, are women. In the south of the country the job is handed down from mother to daughter, but in the north, and as far south as Seoul, where many northern *mudang* fled during the war, they are still chosen by the gods: they may begin to show signs of possession as early as five years old. Present-day *mudang* continue to attain ecstasy while dancing on sharpened blades or pressing them to tongues or throats, and they come to no harm.

The other main manifestation of shamanism in Korea today is in art: engagingly bold, colorful, strongly-outlined depictions of the Ten Symbols of Longevity or the Five Symbols which Repel Evil or the Four Symbols of Good Luck. Longevity symbols, including the

most popular of all, the crane, are used to decorate all manner of household things from celadon cups to embroidered pillow cases. Evil-repelling symbols - dragon, phoenix, tiger, turtle, ox - are most commonly spotted on buildings, where they may adorn roof-tiles, beams or doorways.

CONFUCIANISM

Once a year, on the first Sunday in May, Confucianism has its big splash in central Seoul, when the last surviving members of the royal Yi family, assisted by dozens of priests, musicians and dancers, honor the memories of the royal ancestors enshrined at Chongmyo Shrine. The costumes are gorgeous, the music antique and otherworldly, the dancing mesmerizingly repetitive. Nothing, the visitor is tempted to conclude, could be more exotic, more archaic, more distantly removed from the everyday prob-

The colors of Korea, epitomized ABOVE in the ceiling of the main hall of Tong Myong Burwon temple in Pusan and LEFT in the costumes worn to a contemporary wedding party at central Seoul's Lotte Hotel.

lems of modern Korean life. He could hardly be more wrong.

Confucianism is everywhere in Korea today, scarcely less vigorous and ubiquitous than in the past. The young male foreigner may get his first taste of it at the airport, when the Immigration Officer tells him frankly that he is too young to wear a beard, which is the prerogative of the aged. But that's only the start of it.

If he inquires among the honeymoon couples thronging Cheju-do island, he will discover that all the brides are two,

three or four years younger than their spouses, and that many of the marriages were arranged. Chatting with a young Korean friend at the latter's home he will be surprised at the way his friend extinguishes his cigarette as soon as his father enters the room. The father points out with pride what a good, respectful son he has, for smoking in front of elders is not done. On that Sunday in May at Chongmyo Shrine, after the ceremony, an old man in traditional costume and a long white beard standing near the entrance conducts an apparently hilarious monologue while his middle-aged listeners nod approvingly and youngsters hang on every word. What is he talking about? The Confucian virtues (particularly filial piety), and why they must be kept up.

Confucianism is the moral backbone of Korea, and while the rebellious young may kick against its rigid rules, anyone who remarks approvingly on the honesty, the courtesy, the dignity and the considerateness of Koreans is to a great extent admiring the effects of Confucianism. In China the same code has long been diluted due to that country's greater social mobility and ethnic diversity. In Japan, Confucian behavior persists but its origins are rarely mentioned. Only among Koreans, "the ceremonious people of the East" as the Chinese used to describe them, does it retain its old power, skillfully reinforced by military and industrial hierarchies which find it a matchless way of keeping the game under control.

When Confucianism arrived in the tenth century, it found rich soil in Korea's homogeneous and hierarchical society. Four centuries later, in 1392, Yi Song-gye established the Yi dynasty, and one of his most important reforms was to give official approval to the new, stricter variation of Confucian social ethics and the conservative worldview known now as Neo-Confucianism. Neo-Confucianism froze the social order, made filial piety the ultimate social virtue and required that ancestor worship be the most important religious ceremony in every household. It stressed the supreme importance of harmony and propriety in social relationships, each of which was now governed by specific rules of decorum, or *li*.

The main victims of this ascendancy of Neo-Confucianism were Korean women, and they are still suffering today. In the past, while a new baby boy was lovingly admired on a bed, baby girls were placed on the floor. Girls received no formal education;

ABOVE Bells used during a Confucian ceremony in Seoul. RIGHT Portrait of one of the most eminent of Yi dynasty Confucian scholars, Yi Chae.

they were confined to the home for life, their parents' before marriage and their husbands' afterwards. See-saw jumping was a traditional pastime for girls; it became popular because it afforded them a few brief glimpses of the world beyond the courtyard walls. The only women with any form of social life and personal freedom were the *kisaeng*, who, from the age of fifteen to thirty, enjoyed colorful, sophisticated lifestyles under the patronage of the wealthy, and earned both money and fame. *Kisaeng* were also the only women permitted a proper education, for wit and refinement were essential to their trade. But unlike Chinese sing-song girls and Japanese geisha, *kisaeng* were forbidden to marry their patrons. Once they had lost the bloom of youth they were generally discarded and treated as outcasts, and many became Buddhist nuns.

These gross disparities between the sexes are a thing of the past, and today many Korean women can be found in positions of responsibility. Like their Japanese cousins, however, they remain at the very least half a step behind, and even the ambitious must usually be content with being the power behind the throne rather than on it. But then this is the East, where Taoist ideas of cosmic harmony go even deeper than Confucian social principles; and just as the principles of yin and yang complement each other emblematically on the Korean flag, so most Korean women would probably feel that it is more natural and in keeping with cosmic principles for woman, the yin sex, to complement the aggressive yang role of men than to try to usurp it.

BUDDHISM

Buddhism is not the dominant influence in Korean life that it was before the Yi dynasty reforms, but it is still alive and kicking. Deep in wooded mountains around the country authentic Son (Zen)

masters continue to put their still plentiful students through the most rigorous forms of training. In the cities and towns, temples now defer in number and grandiosity to the modern churches, but the main sects of Buddhism still have millions of adherents, and on paper at least it remains the nation's principal religion.

The extent of popular devotion becomes apparent on Buddha's birthday, the eighth day of the fourth lunar month, when large crowds flock to major temples and hang lanterns to solicit good fortune during the coming year. In Seoul the celebration begins on the preceding evening, when the vast plaza on the island of Yoido, bounded by new skyscrapers, fills with dozens of extraordinary floats - a huge pink lotus flower cradling a small (live) boy, for example, comical-looking dragons with curling silver whiskers sprouting from their nostrils, a number of life-size elephants - which then parade through the city to Chogye temple.

The Mahayana strain of Buddhism first arrived in the peninsula from China in the fourth century, and for a

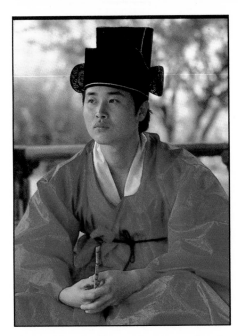

thousand years it was dominant, inspiring all the country's best art, architecture and literature. When Neo-Confucianism arrived in the fourteenth century Buddhism was relegated to the background, but for the mass of people it remained their chief source of spiritual wisdom.

Today there are about 14,000,000 practicing Buddhists and 2,500 temples in Korea. The two major sects are T'aego, which permits marriage among its clergy and currently numbers 2,500 monks and 300 nuns nationwide, and the dominant Chogye sect, which requires that its 8,000 monks and 5,000 nuns be celibate.

CHRISTIANITY

One of the most remarkable things about traveling around Korea is the number of churches one sees. They are everywhere. The smallest village has its pretty, slim, galvanized iron spire; the approach road to the famous Pulguk-sa temple near Kyongju features a solid stone church with a tower that would not look totally out of place in the English Cotswolds. The cities are studded with much grander efforts, many ambitiously modernistic, many still under construction, and in between, as if churches alone were insufficient evidence of the spiritual balance of power, you see dozens of miniature Eiffel Towers holding up huge, neon-lit crosses. This profoundly alien religion, which has barely established a foothold in neighboring Japan, is well dug in here. The Bible is said to be the second most widely-read book in the land after the Chinese classic, the *Romance of the Three Kingdoms*.

Curiously, the first Christian missionary to arrive in Korea from the West came with the Japanese invasion forces sent by Hideyoshi in 1592. He was a Spanish Jesuit named Gregorio de Cespedes, and he accompanied General Konishi, a Christian convert in command of the Christian troops which spearheaded the invasion of the country. Some historians speculate plausibly that Hideyoshi sent them on this desperate mission in order to be rid of them for good. Cespedes had his hands full trying to minister to and maintain the faith of his Japanese flock, and he had no influence on Korean beliefs.

Christianity began to seep into the country from China towards the end of the eighteenth century, and though there were sporadic persecutions, a community of believers was gradually built up, until in 1863 there were twelve Korean priests and some 23,000 believers. Three years later, however, bloody pogroms took place in which nine of the twelve French Catholic missionaries residing in Seoul were publicly beheaded on the banks of the River Han. Over the next three years, some 8,000 of the country's Christians were massacred.

After Korea and the United States signed a diplomatic protocol in 1882,

OPPOSITE Gilt Buddhist image at Chikji-sa Temple, near Taegu. ABOVE Young musician participating in a Confucian ceremony in Seoul.

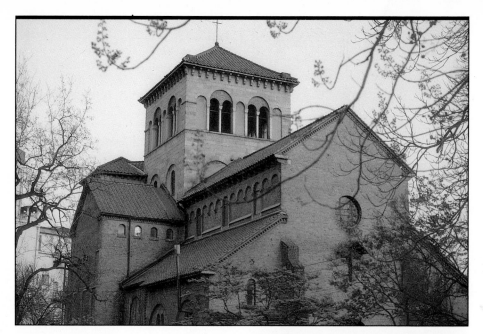

missionaries began to stream into the country, Presbyterians and Methodists being the most successful in attracting followers. At the beginning of the present century Korea was widely regarded as one of the best places in the world for missionary endeavor.

A major reason for the missionaries' success was that they brought all sorts of Western learning with them besides Christianity, and thus attracted many of the most intelligent and energetic into their flocks. They also established the first schools and colleges for women, and when the country was annexed by Japan, missionaries strongly supported the independence effort, which further endeared them to the people at large. The Japanese ended up expelling them en masse in 1940.

Korean Christianity has its own flavor. Many Protestant congregations have a strong evangelical streak, while many Catholic converts show strong tendencies to mysticism - perhaps a reflection of the country's long tradition of shamanism.

Today there are more than eight million Christians in Korea, of whom

some eighty per cent are Protestant. While Christians account for only about twenty per cent of the population, they include many leaders of the intellectual

Early bastions of Christianity in Seoul, TOP the Anglican Cathedral in Chong Dong, the city's original foreign quarter; ABOVE the interior of St Mary's Cathedral in Myong Dong. RIGHT Nuns enjoying the Seoul spring.

and governing èlite, and so have a disproportionately strong influence on the country's affairs.

ARTS AND CRAFTS

A good way into the soul of a people is through the things it makes: the shapes, forms and textures it prizes, the objects it lives among, the sort of spaces it feels at home with.

After an interlude when everything is merely bizarre, the traveler in Korea soon gets on the wavelength of Korean taste: the coarse, cool, fragrant hemp preferred for traditional summer clothing; the naive ebullience of the bright pinks, yellows and blues of girls' ballooning dresses; the subtle blue-greens of celadon pots; the rich amber color of *ondol* floors, the speckled, off-white hand-made paper lining walls and ceilings, the deep varnish and heavy, decorative locks and hinges of old chests.

Korean taste is peculiar and distinctive. Wave after wave of alien influence has washed through the peninsula down the centuries, but Korea has never yet been swamped by it. Homogeneity and the nation's deeply-rooted identity have given Koreans fine, unconscious discrimination. What they have retained is what they are comfortable with.

Korean traditional costume, for example, *hanbok* in Korean, still commonly seen all over the country, is worlds away from that of either China or Japan. Something about the dress of the Mongols, who controlled the country for a bare century, and whose princesses bore three Korean kings, proved agreeable, and the taste stuck. The short waistcoats, jackets tied at the chest with tape, baggy trousers tied at the ankle and generous skirts all reflect Mongol influence. The outfit for men of the aristocratic *yangban* class was traditionally topped off with a stiff, broad-brimmed horsehair hat, while both sexes wore narrow, boat-shaped shoes.

ABOVE The enormous Emille bell, to which a sad story attaches, outside the National Museum in Kyongju. RIGHT Famous eighteenth century painting of a Korea tiger; artist unknown.

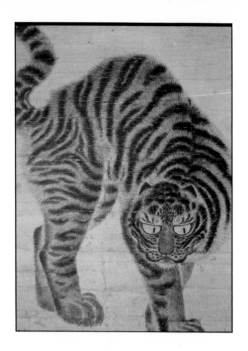

ARCHITECTURE: HUGGING THE GROUND

Korean architecture is also unique, combining the size and solidity of Chinese architecture with the floor-oriented interiors and sliding doors of Japan. The most distinctive thing about the traditional Korean home is the *ondol* heating system, which has been around for thousands of years. Hot air is conducted from a kitchen stove or small underground fireplace to a network of pipes beneath the floor, which is heavily papered and thickly varnished (unless they are up-to-date and use linoleum). Once warm, the temperature can be maintained day and night at minimal expense. Obviously this form of heating is most effective when one is in contact with the floor, whether sitting or lying down - which is one reason why the Koreans declined to move off the floor and on to chairs, as the Chinese had done by the twelfth century. Little furniture is required if you live on the floor, and living-spaces feel larger from that vantage-point; and Korean rooms remain small and snug to this day.

The inspiration for the sort of heavy, black-tiled roofs that were ubiquitous in Korea until the arrival of Western influence was Chinese - but down the centuries the Koreans rang their own changes on the Chinese form. Chinese roofs sweep giddily upward, emphasizing the vertical axis. Korean roofs have a gentler upward tilt at the corners and the buildings themselves hug the ground. Until very recently all dwellings were single-story, another reason why the word "earthy" is one used so frequently in connection with things Korean.

The interiors of traditional Korean rooms are not as cluttered and ornate as those of China, but they are cozy enough in their own way. The space may be divided by a delicate folding screen, decorated with calligraphy or a painting. The low table may be lacquered, and there will be brightly embroidered floor cushions to sit on, besides the wooden chests where bedding is stored during the day. Not only the walls and ceilings but also the sliding doors and windows are covered with hand-made paper, which makes surprisingly good insulation. The framework of the window is carved in complex geometrical patterns.

This sort of interior is found in ideal form only in truly traditional houses, which are now quite rare. In common with the rest of the East, most Koreans have gone over to Western armchairs and sofas in a big way; the old folding-screen may now find itself jammed behind the stereo, while floors are carpeted and windows glazed like anywhere else. *Ondol* heating, however, will probably be retained, and even in a middle-class house in Seoul there is likely to be at least one room with amber floors, embroidered cushions and chests. As this is also the room with the TV in it, it's a sure bet that this is where the master of the house prefers to spend his time off - and the mistress,

too, for the old days when the sexes had separate and almost inviolable territories have gone for good.

The paper used with such versatility in the Korean home has a long history. Introduced from China about a thousand years ago, its manufacture was perfected in Korea, and even today handmade Korean paper is prized by Chinese and Japanese calligraphers for its durability and special absorbent qualities. Paper for windows, screens and *ondol* floors, as well as for painting and calligraphy, is still made by hand in the city of Chonju.

CERAMICS: "ONE OF THE WONDERFUL THINGS"

Ceramics is another area of traditional Korean excellence. Most famous of all, and much imitated by Korean potters today, is the celadon porcelain produced during the Koryo period. "Celadon" refers to an iron-bearing glaze used by the craftsmen of that period to produce pottery of uncannily beautiful blue-green shades. Although the celadon technique was Chinese in origin, Korean craftsmen produced colors of a peculiar subtlety which the Chinese admired greatly but proved unable to reproduce. A Chinese scholar of the Sung period declared that this mysterious color was one of the 10 most wonderful things in the world – the other nine all being Chinese.

The dictionary says celadon means "willow-green," but expert eyes can distinguish over 60 different shades of this subtle color, from a very light yellowish green to an almost brown hue. The most prized shades are "kingfisher-blue," "sky blue after rain," and "sea water washed by rain and wind." By the mid-twelfth century, Koreans had developed their own unique inlay method, whereby designs were inscribed into the wet clay, then the entire piece smeared with soft white clay. When the excess white clay was wiped away from the surface, the inlaid designs remained filled with white. The piece was then glazed with celadon and fired.

Not only the colors but the frank,

LEFT Five-story pagoda of temple in Songni-san National Park. ABOVE Some of the dozens of structures of Pulguk-sa Temple, near Kyongju.

simple designs and the elegant, flowing lines of the Koryo period celadon vases and wine vessels have drawn the admiration of collectors down the ages. Unfortunately the technique by which Korean potters created those mysterious colors was lost in the Mongol invasion, and though modern potters reproduce the old shapes well enough, the colors cannot compare.

When the Yi dynasty was established in 1392, Korean porcelain underwent significant changes. Yi craftsmen were best known for their delicate white porcelain, which was produced exclusively for the court and the nobility. The cruder, more boldly colored and designed ware called *punch'ong* was for the use of commoners, though Japanese connoisseurs were later to fall in love with its frankness and spontaneity, and most of the tea bowls which change hands in Japan for fabulous sums belong to this humbler tradition. The Chinese, on the other hand, set great store by Yi porcelain, and in 1424 the Chinese emperor himself, Yungle, requested some samples for his personal collection.

Like much else in the country's cultural life, ceramics was badly affected by the invasions of the Japanese and the Manchus in the sixteenth century. So impressed were the Japanese by the work of Korea's potters that whole villages of them were carted off and set to work in Japan. It was a compliment of sorts, but the consequence was an impoverishment of ceramics in Korea itself from which the country is only now recovering.

MUSIC AND DANCE: ECSTATIC AND SPONTANEOUS

One of the nicest things about Korea is the way people sing and dance unselfconsciously, whenever and wherever the fancy takes them. Drinkers sing uproariously in bars, beating time with chopsticks; parties of students in the next room at your country inn sing soberly and tunefully, though they don't let up till four in the morning. Girlfriends walking hand in hand down the main streets of Seoul chirp prettily as if they had the world to themselves. Parties of tourists from the country beat drums and prance at the first opportunity after de-bussing, and if you are in the vicinity and show even a glimmer of interest they will catch you up and get you dancing, too. The roots of Korean music and dance are in shamanistic *kut* rituals first performed thousands of years back, and down the ages something ecstatic and spontaneous has happily been retained.

These old shamanistic traditions were taken up and developed during the Shilla era by the *hwarang* ("flower youth"), an exclusive association of noble warriors selected for their looks, martial valor and artistic talents. To these native traditions were added certain music and dance forms from central Asia, which entered Korea along with Buddhism during the Shilla period. During the Yi dynasty music and dance were actively sponsored by the royal court and became important elements in the repertoire of *kisaeng*. For the first time, music and dance were classified and given standard forms, and Yi court officials compiled a "book of dance" as well as a "book of music." Outside the court, the Yi era was also a flourishing time for folk dancing.

During the twentieth century, many traditional Korean dances were corrupted or supplanted by Western styles brought in by the Japanese during their occupation of the country. The last great master of traditional dance was Han Sung-jin, who died in 1938. But with the cultural renaissance currently taking place throughout Korea, traditional native forms are once again being revived.

OPPOSITE TOP LEFT Baskets on display at the Folk Village in Suwon; BELOW silk being spun at another part of the same village; TOP RIGHT dragon-shaped celadon wine pot, from the twelfth century.

Korean music and dance differ significantly from the Western tradition. For one thing, in Korea the two almost always go together. For another, there are no strict rules of choreography and no rigorous formal techniques which must be perfected and repeated exactly at every performance. Spontaneity and improvisation rather than strict adherence to set forms are the crucial points in both music and dance. Instead of telling a story, Korean dance strives to evoke moods and convey feelings. The two key concepts are *hung* (the inner feeling or mood) and *mut* (charm, grace, spiritual inspiration), and their realization depend on the performer's inner resources rather than technique pure and simple.

In Korean dance, arm and upper torso movements are of central importance, while the feet generally remain concealed beneath billowing floor-length robes. Fluid, curving, continuous motions are emphasized, and dancers rarely pause to strike poses. The flowing costumes further enhance the fluidity of Korean dance, and performers often appear to float rather than step across the stage.

Korean dance takes three major forms, court, religious and folk. Traditional court dances were performed by male dancers as well as royal *kisaeng* for the entertainment of the royal family and their retinue - commoners never had a chance to see them. There were two distinct types, *hyang-ak* (of Korean origin) and *t'ang-ak* (of Chinese origin). While the steps were relatively simple, the costumes were highly elaborate. The most popular form was *Hwanganmu,* the "flower crown dance," so named for the small sparkling crown worn by the performers.

Religious dances also came in three distinct types: shaman, Buddhist and Confucian. Shaman dances, usually performed by

RIGHT Eclectically decorated fan, used in Shamanistic ceremony on the east coast; ABOVE Dyana Sect painting from Pomosa Temple, near Pusan.

female *mudang*, were central to the *kut*, and were used both to invoke the spirits and to launch the *mudang* into a trance. Buddhist dances were used to entreat Buddhist deities to smooth the way for departed souls on their journey to heaven. Confucian dances were highly ceremonious forms originally derived from China. They are distinguished, as one might expect, by stiff movements and rigid adherence to form. They still can be seen twice a year in spring and autumn, at Sungkyungkwan University, and once a year, on the first Sunday in May, at the Confucian

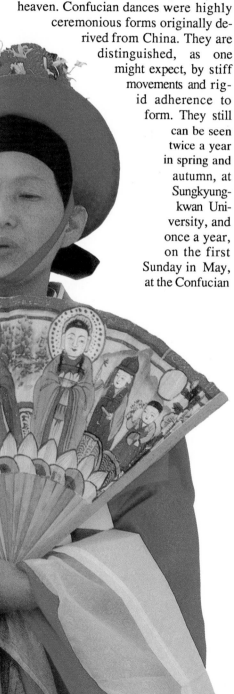

Ceremonies held at Chongmyo Royal Shrine in Seoul.

The most quintessential Korean dances are the folk forms, which retain strong shamanistic overtones. It is in these dances that the idea of expressing inner emotions through outward gestures is most apparent. The oldest and most popular folk dance is the Farmer's Dance, in which the performers spin madly about the stage or floor to the urgent rhythms of drums and gongs. The Farmer's Dance is still performed as a shamanistic rite to purify dwellings, entreat the kindness of benevolent spirits, and exorcise evil forces.

Korea's most distinctive folk dance is the mask-dance drama, which usually satirizes the human frailty of monks and aristocrats. The vividly painted masks are expressive and grotesque. Made of wood, gourd or papier-mâché, they were traditionally burned after each performance in the belief that after use they became contaminated by spirits. Some survived, however, and still serve as models for contemporary mask-makers.

The mask-dance drama served as a folk outlet for the expression of popular resentment against a corrupt clergy and a grasping and oppressive ruling-class. Lechery was the most popular theme, and obscene remarks flew back and forth during the performances. Flutes, cymbals and drums provided the accompaniment. *Bongsan* is the title of the most popular of these dance-dramas.

Among Korea's folk dances, the most powerfully expressive are the solo forms known as *sungmu* and *salpuri*. The *sungmu*, or Buddhist Priest Dance, enacts the seduction of a monk renowned for his chastity by a *kisaeng*, Hwang Chin-I, who was famous for her talent at this sort of thing. Swaying before the monk's cave while beating a beguiling rhythm on her drum, the *kisaeng* brought the show to a climax

51

by dropping her robes to the ground, completing the confusion of the now urgently panting monk. That's how the story goes. In the dance which has developed from this legendary incident, a solo performer appears on stage in baggy, hooded monk's garb, with sleeves that trail along the floor. Fraught with indecision he dances around a large drum, symbolizing the sensual temptation presented by the *kisaeng.* Unable to resist any longer, he suddenly whips a pair of bamboo sticks from his robe and proceeds to play a highly spirited drum solo. The quality of the *sungmu* dance depends entirely on the performer's *hung* and *mut.* If he's in the mood and has the inspiration, this can be the most moving and and expressive of all Korean folk dances.

Korean music obeys a five-note scale, which is why it often sounds out of tune to Western ears accustomed to the seven-note scale. While it has no systematic harmony, its melodies can be striking, with many shifts in rhythm and meter, bold runs, sudden pauses and exquisite undertones. Among the most popular traditional instruments are the *changgo,* a drum shaped like an hour-glass; the *kayagum,* a zither with 12 silk strings; the *p'iri,* a shrill bamboo pipe with a doublereeded mouthpiece; a bamboo flute known as the *taegum;* and chimes of both metal and stone.

Another interesting performing art, one which depends almost entirely on the performer's voice, is the *p'ansori,* a type of narrative told through song. Accompanied only by a barrel drum, the performer sings popular folk-tales in a strong, dramatic voice which conveys the mood quite as well as the meaning of the story. For a full appreciation of this form, it is a good idea to familiarize yourself with the story to be performed beforehand.

While Korean music and dance can be enjoyed almost anywhere and at any time of day or night, the most polished

performances are to be caught at venues such as the Sejong Cultural Center and the National Theater. Korea House and Seoul's top theater-restaurants are also places where professional performances can be enjoyed.

KOREAN MEDICINE

Apart from big ships, blue jeans and running shoes, the export item most closely associated with Korea is ginseng. Known as *insam* in Korean or "manroot," owing to its often uncanny resemblance to the human form, ginseng has been exported from Korea to China and Japan for at least 1,500 years. It is the most visible and well-known member of a huge body of traditional medicines, part of an ancient body of medical scholarship and practice, by means of which Koreans have been protecting themselves from disease since antiquity.

The theory and practice of traditional

Drumming is fundamental to Korean music and dance, whether it's in a farming ritual on Chindo Island ABOVE or at a traditional inn in central Seoul RIGHT.

herbal medicine were already ancient arts in China and Korea at the dawn of written history. Prior to that, herbal medicine was the domain of shamans, who experimented with the medicinal properties of plants, minerals and animal products and passed this hard-earned knowledge on to their successors. The Chinese characters for "medicine" and "doctor" first appeared some 3,000 years ago, marking the transition from shaman healers to professional physicians and pharmacists.

The principles of Chinese medicine were introduced into the court of Koguryo in the year 561. This knowledge quickly spread to the neighboring Paekche and Shilla kingdoms, where it blended with native Korean folk wisdom to create a hybrid medical art. Traditional Korean medicine, *hanyak*, was born from this marriage.

Hanyak continued to develop rapidly during the Koryo dynasty, and during the Yi era, an age of scholarship, Korean medical manuals and pharmacopoeias began to appear in great profusion. Over the centuries much of this Chinese and Korean medical knowledge filtered into Japan, where it formed the basis for traditional medicine there.

Korean medicine reached its zenith in 1610 with the publication of a massive 25-volume Korean pharmacopoeia called *Tong-I Pogam (Treasures of Eastern Medicine)*. Compiled and written over a period of 16 years by the court physician Ho Jun, this comprehensive and remarkably accurate medical manual is still used today by herbal doctors and pharmacists throughout the Orient.

Despite fierce competition from *yak-guk* (Western medicine), *hanyak* continues to thrive throughout Korea. Herbal shops in Seoul and elsewhere still stock everything from chrysanthemum petals for headaches and rhemannia root for heart ailments, to snake wine for impotence and dried tortoise for lumbago.

Acupressure massage, acupuncture, moxibustion, pulse diagnosis, herbal diets, calisthenics, deep-breathing and other aspects of the great East Asian medical tradition also continue to flourish in modern Korea, primarily because Western medicine has proved incapable of coping with many of man's most troublesome ailments.

The difference between Western and traditional Eastern attitudes to the medical profession is instructive. In ancient Korea, families used to retain a doctor to supervise the health of its members, much as modern American corporations retain attorneys. The doctor would visit the family regularly, dispensing herbal prescriptions and medical advice and watching for signs of weakness or disease in each patient's health. Should a member of the family fall seriously ill, the doctor was held responsible for not preventing it, and all payment to him ceased. The doctor was then obliged to cure the patient – at his own expense! Only when he succeeded did payments resume. If he failed he lost an entire family of patients, as well as a lot of face. Under such a system it is hardly surprising that preventive medicine made great strides.

Prevention is at the heart of Korean and Chinese medicine. A patient's overall condition is analyzed in the light of such diverse factors as the functional inter-relationships between his organs, his emotional life, his immediate physical environment, his diet, his sexual habits, the weather, the season and the local geography. Once the doctor has studied all these factors to obtain a complete picture of the patient's condition, he then prescribes herbal supplements, offers dietary advice and applies a variety of therapeutic methods to compensate for deficiencies, suppress

OPPOSITE A sidewalk peddler of traditional herbal medicines evidently enjoying his role.

excesses, adjust malfunctions, and generally help the patient to balance his entire system for optimum health.

Balance and harmony are the key concepts in traditional Eastern medicine. The most basic balance involves the dual cosmic forces of Yin and Yang; Yang energy is aggressive ascending, hot, bright and male; Yin energy is passive, descending, cool, dark and female. A sudden outburst of temper, for example, generates excess Yang energy in the liver, which rises to the heart and head, causing dizziness, headaches, heat and fatigue. Cooling Yin herbs alleviate the discomfort of Yang excess and restore the correct balance with Yin energy. Listlessness and ennui, on the other hand, might be attributed to an excess of Yin energy, which tends to slow down the system and depress vital bodily functions. In this case, warming and stimulating Yang herbal prescriptions are called for. The key to curing ailments caused by yin-yang energy imbalance is to reestablish the proper balance between the two.

Herbal potions are one way of doing this; another, widely practiced in Korea as in China and Japan, is acupuncture. Acupuncture is based on the concept of *ki*, variously translated "vital energy," "life-force" or "breath." *Ki* is perhaps the greatest stumbling-block to the West's reaching an understanding of the Eastern medical tradition, for Western doctors simply do not acknowledge its existence. According to ancient Chinese theories, *ki* is the vital life-energy that animates all living things. It flows through the body along a complex, invisible network of lines called meridians that feed the body with vital energy much as the circulatory system feeds the cells with blood. When *ki* is stagnant or otherwise unable to flow along its normal course through the meridians due to disease or traumatic shock, the organs and other parts of the body fed by that meridian begin to suffer and degenerate. An acupuncture needle inserted into a vital point along the blocked meridian clears the obstacle and causes *ki* to surge along that channel, pouring vital energy into the affected parts of the body.

THE MANY GUISES OF GINSENG

So where does ginseng fit in? Ginseng is the substance which is most intimately associated with traditional Korean medicine. Korea has long been recognized as the most important source of the root, and when a tributary relationship was established with China, ginseng was one of the main items sent annually to the Chinese court.

The use of ginseng as a medicine goes back to the origins of Eastern medical history, for it appeared in prescriptions in the *Nei Ching*, the first Chinese manual of medicine. Originally sought in the wild mountain recesses of Korea and Manchuria, ginseng is now cultivated on a large scale in Korea. You'll see it growing in many places around the country; it is readily spotted on account of the long, neat rows of low thatch shelters which protect this sensitive plant from sun, wind and rain.

Cultivating ginseng is a painstaking process requiring constant care. The roots grow to maturity in four to six years. After harvesting, they are washed, peeled, steamed and dried, then sorted according to age and quality. The roots so deplete the soil of nutrients that nothing will grow where they have been cultivated for several years - but this absorption process is the source of the root's great potency. The root has a vital role in Korea's economy, in addition to the vital role it plays in the nation's medical arts, and exports of ginseng and related products earn Korea hundreds of millions of dollars in foreign exchange every year.

The variety of products currently made with ginseng is mind-boggling.

Ginseng roots come in many shapes. If appearance helps stimulate the appetite this suggestive specimen will be much prized.

Besides the root itself, you can now purchase ginseng pills, powder, extract, candy, chewing gum, jam, tea, wine, skin cream, soap, shampoo, even ginseng cigarettes. Recent scientific studies have confirmed its efficacy as a general tonic as well as a specific cure for many common ailments. Its primary pharmacodynamic effects include stimulation of the central nervous system, increased mental awareness and physical stamina, improved appetite and digestion, elimination of chronic fatigue and hangovers, and enhanced metabolism. It sounds like a panacea, but this does not mean its effects are immediate. Ginseng is most beneficial when taken in small, regular doses over a long period of time.

Ginseng comes in two varieties, white (*baek*) and red (*hong*). The white variety is more common and less expensive, and is generally available throughout Korea as well as overseas. The red variety is considerably more potent and at least four times as expensive, and most of the production is reserved for the lucrative export market, where demand for it continues to rise. For most people and purposes, however, white ginseng is perfectly suitable, especially if properly administered over a long period of time. Red ginseng, with its greater concentrations of active ingredients, is best for weak, aged or seriously ill patients.

Despite the proliferation of newfangled ginseng products, a traditional infusion of the dried root remains the best and most pleasant way to take it. *Insam cha jip* (ginseng tea houses) abound in Korea, readily identified by the large ginseng root painted on the door and the pungent aroma of herbal brews wafting from within. A variety of ginseng and other herbal teas are available in these places, which are popular for relaxing and chatting after a meal. The most traditional ginseng brew consists of white ginseng root, dried jujubes (so-called "Chinese dates") and pine nuts, boiled together with a little sugar. Drunk as a tonic stimulant, this potion increases potency and physical strength, improves the circulation and promotes an efficient metabolism. Ginger tea *(saeng kang cha)* is brewed from ginger root and raw sugar, and is highly recommended for fighting chills and preventing colds in winter. Various other health-giving concoctions are available. All are made by boiling the herbal ingredients in water with a little raw sugar until the liquid is reduced by about one-third.

Ginseng is strictly controlled by a government monopoly bureau, which oversees every aspect of production and marketing. Quality control is rigorous, and prices are uniform throughout the country. It is sold everywhere in Korea and remains one of the country's best bargains, regardless of its price, for ginseng is a long-term investment in good health.

KOREAN CUISINE

A LUSTY ART

If it's true that you are what you eat, then the vibrant, dynamic nature of the Korean people might well be traced to their diet. The least known of the culinary traditions of Asia, Korean cuisine is the best evidence there is of the nation's cultural distinctiveness.

Almost the only point Korean cuisine shares in common with the cuisines of its larger neighbors – and indeed with the rest of Asia as well – is the vital role played by rice as the primary staple. "Have you eaten rice yet?" is a common greeting in both Chinese and Korean, roughly equivalent to the English "Hi, how are you?" The implication is that if you have then you must be feeling all right; and if you haven't, then you should be offered some food forthwith. First things first!

Koreans eat three full meals a day, and the number of dishes increases with each meal. At least half a dozen dishes appear with the traditional Korean breakfast, twice that number with lunch, and 20 or more at a full-scale banquet in the evening. Short grain rice is the staple at every meal, in the past often blended with barley or millet to stretch limited supplies. Like the Chinese and the Japanese, Koreans also eat noodles (sautd or in soups), soy beans and bean curd, bean sprouts and red lentils. There the similarities end.

The most popular methods of cooking in Korea are communal "hot-pots" and the grilling of meat over charcoal or gas-fired braziers. Both methods reflect Mongol influence on Korean eating habits, and both permit cooking at one's own table. Traditionally, diners sat on cushions on *ondol* floors around low, lacquered tables, and most Korean restaurants today still feature such charming *ondol* rooms as well as more contemporary table-and-chair set-ups. Implements comprise a long-handled, rather flat metal spoon, used for soups, stews and even rice, and a pair of slender metal chopsticks; dishes include a metal rice bowl with a lid, a soup bowl, and several small saucers for dips and garnishes.

ALL THE KIMCH'I YOU CAN EAT

The undisputed symbol of Korean cuisine is kimch'i, a term which refers to any side-dish which has been pickled in brine with garlic and chilies. There are more than 24 varieties of kim-ch'i, each prepared in an infinite number of

subtly different ways, and at least two or three versions appear with every meal. An old Korean adage has it that "A man can live without a wife, but not without his kimch'i," and only Seoul's most fanatically international restaurants fail to provide it. Practically every home in the country has rows of big black kimch'i pots fermenting away in backyard, porch or balcony.

Chili and garlic are the *sine qua non* of kimch'i; the most basic and widely-encountered variety calls for heads of fresh cabbage to be sliced, salted, placed in brine with plenty of chili and garlic, then set to ferment in those big pots. In summer, when fermentation is rapid and cabbages plentiful, kimch'i is made fresh daily; prior to the onset of winter the kimch'i pots are packed in straw and buried up to their necks in the ground to prevent freezing, then left to ferment for months.

Korean use of garlic goes back to prehistoric times. Chilies, on the other hand, are relative newcomers, having arrived on merchant ships from the Americas during the fifteenth and sixteenth centuries. Korea took to the fiery pods like fish to water.

The following are among the most popular varieties of kimch'i:

sobaegi kimch'i: cabbage stuffed with oysters;
oee sobaegi kimch'i: sliced cucumbers with radish and ginger;
kakdooki kimch'i: diced white radish with scallions;
dong chimi kimch'i: white radish sticks floating in brine.

Besides garlic and chili, favorite Korean seasonings include scallions, ginger, sesame oil, sesame seeds and soy sauce. Cooking herbs, which are applied according to the principles of tra-

A Korean meal is an attractive display and rare is one without at least some of the pickled side-dishes displayed in this lavish banquet setting.

ditional herbal medicine, include wild aster, aralia root, royal fern bracken, shepherd's purse, mugwort and bluebell. There is also a whole range of fermented pastes and sauces for dipping, called *chang*. Every home and restaurant has its own recipe for *chang*, and each batch comes out differently. Based on a fermented mash of soybeans, the three most common varieties are *kan chang*, a dark liquid, like soy sauce, *daen chang*, a thick, pungent paste, and *kochu chang*, a fiery version laced with chilies.

ON THE SIDE: CRAB LEGS AND GREEN GARLIC

The side dishes known as *panch'an* add variety to the basic Korean meal. Popular *panch'an*, which are also served in bars as *anju*, tidbits to accompany drinks, include the following treats:

tubu: soybean curd, tofu;
kejang: raw crab legs marinated in red chili sauce;
saengson hoe: sliced raw fish, sashimi;
myong nan jot: fish roe in garlic sauce;
sigumchi namul: blanched spinach dressed with sesame oil and seeds;
myul chee chorim: dried anchovies sautéd with chili peppers;
saengson yangnyumgui: broiled fish sprinkled with sesame seeds;
manul changah-chee: green garlic pickled in soy sauce;
kul chun: sautéd oysters;
don chun: beef and bean curd patties spiced with ginger;
pindaedok: mung bean pancakes laced with shrimp, "Korean pizza";
sabsanchok: ground-beef patties with garlic and sesame seeds.

SOUPS AND STEWS

Koreans love to blend meat, fish, mollusks and vegetables together to make rich, thick stews, especially in winter. *Kuk* and *tang* are the words for soup, while *chim* and *chongol* refer to stew. *Chigae* is a special thick stew simmered in heavy clay crocks. Favorite Korean soups and stews include the following:

maeun tang: rich soup of meat, fish, bean curd, zucchini and scallions;
dae hap kuk: clam soup;
malgun chang kuk: beef and white radish soup;
saengsun kuk: fish and cabbage soup;
mandu kuk: soup with meat dumplings;
miyok kuk: spinach, radish and seaweed soup;
kalbi chim: stew of beef short ribs;
kungchung chonggol: stew of meat, fish, mollusks and vegetables;
ten chang chigae: thick stew of meat, fish, bean curd, squash and chilies;
piji chigae: thick stew of pork and kimch'i in broth.

The unrivaled star of Korean cuisine is beef, and *bulgogi*, beef finely sliced, and *kalbi*, beef short-ribs, are the most popular ways of eating it. In both cases the meat is marinated in soy sauce, wine, sugar and spices, then grilled at your table on charcoal or gas-fired braziers. For *kalbi*, a small grill is placed over the coals; for *bulgogi*, a metal dome with a moat around the edge to catch the juices is placed over the fire. The dome looks a little like a helmet, and in fact it is said that the Mongol warrior's helmet was the original inspiration for this style of cooking. Grilled beef meals come with rice, assorted kimch'i, sauces for dipping, and fresh lettuce leaves for wrapping morsels of meat with kimch'i, rice and spice to form tasty little dumplings. *Bulgogi-jip* (grilled beef restaurants) abound

TOP Eating out in Korea: the long metal spoons, throwaway chopsticks and dish of kim'chi are ubiquitous, but the small one- or two-person dinner table is becoming rare. Koreans excel in the creation of stews CENTER LEFT AND RIGHT and the preparation of rice, which they may wrap in seaweed *à la Japonaise* BOTTOM LEFT or pound until sticky BOTTOM RIGHT.

throughout Korea, and are readily identified by the round holes set in the center of the tables to accommodate braziers.

A MEAL IN A BOWL

For simpler meals, especially for summer lunches, you could try one of the great Korean "single-bowl" meals. The best-known is *naeng-myon:* noodles of buckwheat or potato flour in cold broth, with sliced cucumber, pear-apple and pressed beef, topped with an egg and accompanied by a choice of seasonings. Other popular Korean noodle meals include the following:

momil kookso: buckwheat noodles with sweet radish sauce;
odaeng kookso: wheat noodles with fish cake in broth;
kong kookso: wheat noodles in fresh soy milk;
chap chae: thin rice noodles sautéd with meat and vegetables;
udong: broad wheat noodles with onions, bean curd, egg and chili.

If you would prefer a rice-based one-bowl meal, try asking for *hanjongshik*, which literally means "the meal of the day." This consists of a bowl of rice served with an array of fresh side dishes and a bowl of pickled cabbage soup. *Kongnamul pap* is a little fancier, with bean sprouts, beef and cabbage served over rice. The king of Korean rice dishes, however, is *pipimpap*, which is as much fun to eat as it is to pronounce. A big bowl of rice is topped with bean sprouts, bluebell root, blanched fern, spinach and a fried egg, and accompanied by a bowl of soup. Just mix it all up with your chopsticks and dig in.

One of the best Korean single-bowl meals is *samgyae tang*, which consists of a whole spring chicken stuffed with rice, white ginseng and dried jujubes, then steamed for hours in its own broth

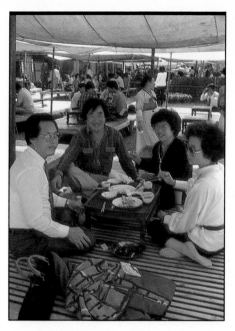

in a heavy iron pot. More than just a meal, this dish is also a potent tonic food.

THE FOOD OF KINGS

There are two dishes, formerly reserved exclusively for Korean royalty, which dedicated gourmets will definitely wish to try while in Korea. *Kujolpan* ("Nine-treasure dish") comes in an octagonal lacquered dish with nine compartments. Delicate crepe skins fill the center compartment, surrounded by the other eight treasures: shredded egg, sautéd cucumbers, onions, mushrooms, beef, carrots, cabbage and shrimp. Just grab a crêpe skin and "roll your own."

The other royal delicacy is *sinsullo*, which comes in a brass pot with a chimney, much like a Mongolian firepot. Sliced beef with chopped onions and seasonings are placed in the bottom, with eggs, carrots, cucumbers, beef liver, chopped beef, blanched walnuts and fried ginko nuts neatly arranged on top. Live coals are then dropped into the chimney, while hot broth is poured over the ingredients. After a brief but vigorous simmering

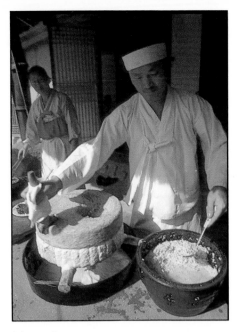

it's ready to eat.

Meals in Korea are usually accompanied by teas of various sorts, mostly teas brewed from grains, dried fruits and ginseng. *Bori cha* (barley tea) is the commonest, and is served and drunk in place of water at every restaurant, coffee-shop and tea-room in the country. *Mogwa cha* (quince tea) and *hodo cha* (walnut tea) are other common varieties. *Insam cha* (ginseng tea) is a tonic drink imbibed the year round by Koreans of all ages. In recent years *kopi* (coffee), too, has become popular.

DRINKING: A NATIONAL PASTIME

Koreans like to drink, and there is no better way for the foreigner to get close to Koreans and find out what they are really thinking than by sharing a few glasses with them in a typical *sul-jip* (bar).

Drinking has always played an important part in Korean life from the King's court downwards, as the fre-

OPPOSITE Culinary time-travel at Suwon's Folk Village. ABOVE an artisan at the Folk Village makes candy in the traditional way.

quent excavation by archaeologists of ancient drinking cups and flasks attests. The ancient literature and painting are also full of boozing, and the habit proved the downfall of one Shilla dynasty king when soldiers from the neighboring Paekche kingdom surprised him and his courtiers during a party. The site at Kyongju, known as Posokjong (abalone bower) may still be viewed.

Drinking parties were formerly an exclusively male preserve, only *kisaeng* being excepted from the rule. This is changing rapidly, however, and Korean women seem to be developing as much of a taste for liquor as men.

Certain elements of traditional Korean etiquette are still observed by Koreans, particularly at formal parties, and foreigners who are clearly familiar with these customs will make a good impression. Never pour your own drink at a banquet, unless you wish to appear crude and greedy. Korean custom requires that you hold your glass before you (preferably with both hands) while your host, neighbor, waiter or *kisaeng* pours your drink for you. If someone toasts you and drains his glass, you are expected to follow suit. In this way many drinkers toast their way to oblivion, and this is absolutely normal and okay. No stigma attaches to drunkenness in Korea.

These are Korea's most popular drinks:

Soju: the common man's tipple, the cheapest and strongest Korean liquor, distilled from sweet potatoes or anything else that comes to hand; a taste which one is well advised not to go to too much trouble acquiring, as it can have a nasty kick the morning after; but goes well with Korean-style sausages and other meat dishes.

Makkolli: a milky, off-white brew, in taste akin to ginger beer, but more potent than it leads you to believe; formerly the nation's most popular drink, but rapidly losing out to beer. *Makolli* pubs, *makolli-jip*, used to be the most popular neighborhood bars, but in the big cities have now largely disappeared. In the countryside, however, they are still common.

Popchu: high-grade, refined *makkolli,* very popular in Kyongju but also available in Seoul.

Chungchong: a high-grade rice wine similar to Japanese sake and usually served hot; a specialty of Kwangju.

Insam-ju: ginseng liquor made by immersing an entire ginseng root in clear rice wine; drunk as a tonic. The best brand is reputedly "Jinro." You can eat the root after you've emptied the bottle.

Paem-sool: another (albeit officially discouraged) potent tonic liquor, made by immersing an entire snake in strong liquor. After drinking, eat the snake.

Maekju (beer): introduced by the Japanese during their occupation, beer has rapidly grown in popularity in recent years. The two local brands, OB and Crown, are very drinkable, and Heineken is now made under license (though it's dear). Bottled beer (*pyong-maekju*) is available at almost every restaurant, roadside stall and cafe in the land. Draft beer (*saeng-maekju*) is served in beer halls as well as in Western hotel and restaurant bars. Another type of beer hall is called *tong-dalk-jip* and specializes in broiled chicken and draft beer.

Yang-ju ("Foreign liquor") is also growing in popularity, especially in Seoul. Due to taxation, imported liquor is exorbitantly expensive, but recently Korea has begun producing its own whiskey, gin, brandy and other drinks with imported ingredients and technology. Of the Korean whiskies currently on the market the best is "Blackstone;" made in collaboration with Chivas Regal, it is surprisingly smooth. A few Western-style grape wines are also on the market, the most palatable being a Riesling called *Ma-ju-ang.*

If you are eating at a Chinese restaurant, you may like to sample the traditional Chinese spirits - but have a care! The strongest of the lot, *baek-gal* ("white and dry"), is a sorghum spirit of incredible potency - around 150 proof. It will leave you breathless and burning, and it intoxicates rapidly. *Kaoliangju* ("sorghum liquor") is similar but rather less fiery. The most interesting Chinese liquor is *o-ga-pi-ju,* a thick, dark liquor blended with potent medicinal herbs, and renowned as a stimulating tonic. It's best taken in winter, for it has remarkable warming properties.

For more concrete suggestions about good places to eat and drink, see **Seoul by Night** and **Traveler's Tips.**

HAN'GUL: GREAT WRITING, VULGAR SCRIPT

Even travelers familiar with other parts of East Asia will be floored at first by Korea's writing system; many of its shapes are naggingly suggestive of Chinese characters, but the principle at work appears to be quite different.

And so it is. *Han'gul,* "the great writing", Korea's own alphabet, was created for the purpose of expressing the sounds of Korean in the simplest yet most comprehensive manner. Five hundred and twenty years after its promulgation, it still does just that.

It really is simple. Here's how it works. Each Korean sound has its own sign, whether vowel, diphthong or consonant. The consonant "K", for example, is represented by the symbol ㄱ, the vowel "I" by the symbol ㅣ, the consonant "M" by the symbol ㅁ. These symbols are the building-blocks of individual syllables. Thus, using the symbols above for "K", "I" and "M" we can put together the most common family name "Kim", as follows: 김.

Han'gul menus are a considerable problem for the foreign visitor, one for which there is no easy solution, but here's how to read (or write) one of the most popular of Korean dishes, *pipimpap.* The first syllable consists of "P", ㅂ and "I", ㅣ and comes out ㅂㅣ. The second consists of "P" and "I" again, and "M", which we already learnt when we were studying how to write "Kim", viz. ㅁ. So "Pim" comes out 빔. The third syllable is made up of "P" again, ㅏ, "A", and "P" once more - in toto, 밥. Put them all together to make *"pipimpap"* and there you are: 비빔밥. It really is as simple as that.

Now you know how the words are constructed, all you have to do is memorize the symbols. Copy the chart below and carry it around with you at all times. Mug it up in spare moments. Within a week or two you will find you can read almost anything, and when you go back home you will be the wonder of your friends, who had no idea you were so intelligent.

Of course, reading is not the same as understanding, and most of the words you laboriously decipher will mean just as little to you as they would have done if you had not bothered. Still, it's an important step in the right direction, and can be of great practical use in restaurants and bus stations.

HAN'GUL: THE BASIC FORTY SYMBOLS

The chart below shows the basic *han'gul* symbols and their romanized equivalents according to the McCune-Reischauer System, which is the most widely used and accepted.

VOWELS CONSO- NANTS	ㅏ [a]	ㅑ [ya]	ㅓ [o]	ㅕ [yo]	ㅗ [o]	ㅛ [yo]	ㅜ [u]	ㅠ [yu]	ㅡ [u]	ㅣ [I]
ㄱ [kg]	가	갸	거	겨	고	교	구	규	그	기
ㄴ [n]	나	냐	너	녀	노	뇨	누	뉴	느	니
ㄷ [t, d]	다	댜	더	뎌	도	됴	두	듀	드	디
ㄹ [r, l]	라	랴	러	려	로	료	루	류	르	리
ㅁ [m]	마	먀	머	며	모	묘	무	뮤	므	미
ㅂ [p, b]	바	뱌	버	벼	보	뵤	부	뷰	브	비
ㅅ [s, h]	사	샤	서	셔	소	쇼	수	슈	스	시
ㅇ [*]	아	야	어	여	오	요	우	유	으	이
ㅈ [ch, j]	자	쟈	저	져	조	죠	주	쥬	즈	지
ㅊ [ch']	차	챠	처	쳐	초	쵸	추	츄	츠	치
ㅋ [k']	카	캬	커	켜	코	쿄	쿠	큐	크	키
ㅌ [t']	타	탸	터	텨	토	툐	투	튜	트	티
ㅍ [p']	파	퍄	퍼	펴	포	표	푸	퓨	프	피
ㅎ [h]	하	햐	허	혀	호	효	후	휴	흐	히

The History of *Han'gul*

The art of writing reached Korea from China, and as late as the fifteenth century all Korean law, literature and history - everything that required literary expression - was written in Chinese ideograms. Elegant and complex, each character carried its own meaning, and so the Chinese system proved an effective means of communication between countries with different languages: though each could make no sense at all of the noises the other made, once the idea was put down in ideograms they could understand each other very well.

Chinese was, however, much less suitable for Koreans to use when addressing each other: the huge number of ideograms meant that only a leisured elite could master the system, and the sentence structure of Chinese was also quite different from Korean. By the fifteenth century this stubborn problem presented itself so forcibly to King Sejong, fourth and greatest ruler of the Yi dynasty, that he set about solving it. He put a committee of the nation's greatest scholars to work in the Hall of Talented Scholars in the grounds of Kyongbok Palace, and three years later he was able to publish the fruits of their labor. As he stated at the time,

> "Being distinct from Chinese, the Korean language is not confluent with Chinese characters. Hence, those who have something to put into words are unable to express their feelings. To overcome such distressing circumstances, I have designed ... letters that everyone may learn with ease and use with convenience in their daily life."

Initially, conservative Confucian scholars vigorously opposed the new writing system, claiming that it would offend "Great China" by "dragging the Chinese classics in the dust of vulgar script." In a petition to the throne presented in 1444, the academician Choe Mal-li protested, "If these graphs should flow into China, and if people there should adversely criticize them, how could we be without shame? Only types such as the Mongolians, Tanguts, Jurchen, Japanese and Tibetans have their own graphs, but these are matters for the barbarians..."

Fortunately for Korea, King Sejong persisted in his mission, and sparked enough interest among more enlightened scholars to prevent the *han' gul* from passing away in its infancy. In established literary circles, however, it remained subordinate to Chinese characters until the arrival of Christian missionaries in the nineteenth century. They were quick to see the merits of *han' gul* as a tool for disseminating knowledge to the masses, and as a result of their lead it soon became the universal way of representing the language. *Han' gul* survived suppression by the Japanese occupation, and nowadays is ubiquitous. Chinese ideograms are still taught in school and understood by all Koreans with a claim to culture, but their use in everyday life is very limited.

See **Travelers' Tips** for a list of basic Korean words and phrases, and for a note on romanization.

THE SEOUL OLYMPICS

There is little doubt that September 17, to October 2, 1988 will be the two most important weeks in the Republic of Korea's history to date. That's when some 13,000 athletes and officials, 9,000 journalists, 7,000 delegates and 270,000 foreign spectators are expected to descend on Seoul for the 24th Olympic Games.

It was in 1981 that the International Olympic Committee decided that the next Olympics after Los Angeles should go to Seoul, and the country has been undergoing paroxysms of preparation ever since. The capital's substrata has

been riddled with subway tunnels which now cover 116.5 km (72 miles) and one of the lines connects the Seoul Sports Complex, major venue for the Games, with the city center. The already well-developed expressway network was expanded and now one may travel from Seoul to anywhere in the country and be back in the capital the same day. A number of the stadiums and other facilities needed for the Games were already built and in use by 1981, but 15 new ones had to be constructed from scratch, including the huge main

stadium of the Sports Complex, designed by celebrated Korean architect Kim Swoo-gun and opened in 1984. The finished complex comprises a baseball stadium, indoor swimming pool, two gymnasiums and a warm-up field in addition to the main stadium. It occupies an area of 54.5 hectares (135 acres) and has an overall capacity of 200,000. The main stadium alone can accommodate 100,000.

Seoul's other main venue, the Olympic Park, occupies a vast area four kilometers (two and a half miles) east of the complex along the south bank of the Han River and accommodates a velodrome, tennis courts, weightlifting and fencing gyms, a gymnastic hall, and an indoor swimming pool with a profile strongly suggestive of Admiral Yi's famous Turtle Ships. The Olympic and Press village will be located here, and there will be about 50 hectares (135 acres) of greenery in the total area of 291 hectares (719 acres).

Seoul is very decidedly Korea's capital, and most of the Olympic events not scheduled for the Complex or the Park

major cities, Taegu, Kwangju and Taejon, will also host some events.

Besides the Games themselves, an ambitious Festival of Arts and Culture will be held around and during those weeks in autumn '88, including performances of Korean court and folk dance and music, concerts of Western classical music and exhibitions of Korean art treasures.

One of the biggest headaches for the organizers of the Olympics has been how to put up all the visitors. Already Seoul has 54 hotels of at least

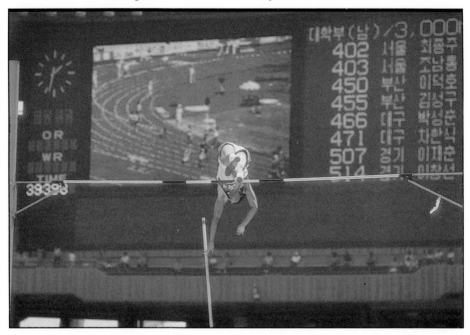

will take place in other venues in the center or suburbs of the capital. The regatta course, for example, is on the Han River, 30 km (18.5 miles) east of Seoul; the modern pentathlon will take place in Taenung Country Club in the northeast of the city, while judo events will be held in Yong-In, an hour's drive to the south. A few events will be staged in other cities, however. Pusan, the nation's second city, will be the site of yachting events, and a mammoth coastal site is being built for that purpose. The municipal stadiums of the other

decent tourist standard, with over 12,000 rooms; by the time of the Games, some 13 new ones will be in operation, with 4,000 rooms between them. Even so, a huge shortfall is anticipated, and to help fill the breach many local hotels and *yogwan* will be encouraged to upgrade their facilities to make them more suitable for foreign visitors. In addition, every available

OPPOSITE Participant in the opening ceremony of Seoul's Olympic Stadium. ABOVE Athlete in the National Games putting in some practice for '88. OVERLEAF Panoramic view of the spectacular opening of the Asian Games in 1986.

type of housing, including condominiums, apartments, school dormitories and even private homes, will be pressed into service. There was even talk at one time of mooring a large ship at the port of Inch'on, and boarding surplus visitors there.

Koreans have been eager participants in the Olympics for decades. A Korean, Sohn Kee-chung, won the marathon at Berlin in 1936, running for Japan, and since 1948, when they first took part under their own flag, they have done consistently well in boxing, weightlifting, judo, and more recently in wrestling, basketball, volleyball and archery as well. In Los Angeles they gave their best collective performance ever, ranking tenth in the final tally and collecting 19 medals.

A political shadow hangs over the Olympics as it hangs over all Korea's international activities, and at the time of writing it was not clear to what extent the participation of the Eastern bloc countries in the Games could be anticipated. As a sop to North Korean feelings the suggestion has been made that some of the events might be held there.

Even if the Games are only a partial success in this respect, however, it will still have done great things for Korea's image and place in the world. The 1964 Tokyo Olympics, the only previous Games to be held in Asia, marked and was in large part responsible for a huge turnaround both in the world's attitude toward Japan and Japan's attitude to the rest of the world: once again the country seemed to have become part of the world community. The Seoul Olympiad is likely to have a similar effect. If it does, the US$2.25 billion it is likely to cost may be considered money well spent.

Official competitions will be held in 23 sports and demonstrations in two

others. Of the official sports, tennis and table tennis are new additions to the Olympic Games. The schedule of events is printed on the last page of this guide.

SPORT IN KOREA

The Olympics aside, sports of all kinds enjoy huge popularity in Korea, and the nation has made its impact felt in many international competitions. In particular, the reputation Koreans enjoy as one of the feistiest of Asian peoples is substantiated by their success in the martial arts, both eastern and western.

The indigenous martial art is *T'aekwondo,* "the Way of Feet and Fists," which has been practiced in the peninsula for the best part of 2,000 years. It's an explosively dynamic fighting system in which the contestants concentrate all their energy, mental as well as physical, on assaulting carefully identified spots on the opponent's body. *T'aekwondo* is related to but distinct from both Chinese kung-fu and Okinawan karate and has in recent years gained wide international recognition. Now there are schools with Ko-

ABOVE Grecian wrestling at the National Games. Koreans excel in many of the martial arts, Western as well as Eastern, and embrace baseball OPPOSITE enthusiastically.

rean instructors dotted all over the globe. Koreans continue to win the majority of the titles at the regular international championships in which teams from more than sixty nations compete, and the sport has become one of the official events at the Asian Games. If you want to see a demonstration of the sport, contact the **World T'aekwondo Federation** at its headquarters in Kukkiwon, in the southern suburbs of Seoul, where regular exhibition bouts are staged. Call 776-2347 or 777-6080/9 for further information.

Yudo, judo to you, is the other oriental fighting art which has Korea in its grip. The "Way of Gentleness" was introduced into Korea from China in 1150, after which the Koreans taught it to the Japanese and then for many centuries lost interest in it. The Japanese brought it back with them during their occupation, and it is once again popular nationwide. It is part of the compulsory training of Korean policemen. It's not the only form of wrestling the Koreans go in for. *Ssirum,* a sport introduced by the Mongols, requires the hefty contestants to throw each each other to the

ground, employing a strictly limited repertoire of trips, twists and flips; it bears a passing resemblance to Japanese sumo, and may often be seen at spring and autumn country festivals. Western-style wrestling has also had a large following since the Koreans took a gold for that event (featherweight free-style) at the 1976 Olympics. And boxing, where Koreans have excelled in the lighter categories for many years, approaches the status of a national sport.

The two most popular ball games in Korea are soccer and baseball. Baseball was professionalized several years ago, and the razzmatazz of the present-day game, and the long hours of television exposure it commands, are strongly reminiscent of the situation over the water in Japan. Koreans have been playing soccer ever since 1882, when the crew of a visiting British warship gave a demonstration of how it was done, and on both sides of the DMZ it is played avidly and with great skill. Both North and South Korean teams have in the past done remarkably well in the World Cup.

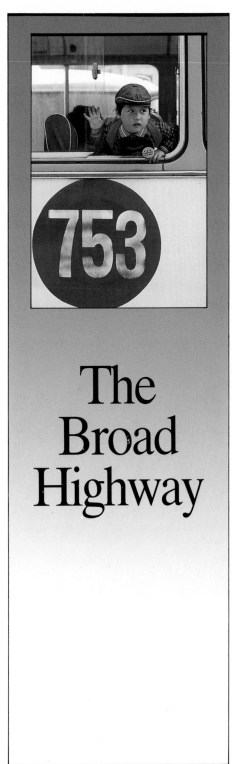

The
Broad
Highway

SEOUL: CAPITAL CITY

Seoul is not only the capital of Korea, by far the largest and most important city. It is also the heart of the nation's contemporary life and an expansive open-air museum of its past, the only city in the Republic where enough has been preserved from the successive epochs that the alert visitor can, in the space of a few days, gain a keen sense of Korea's continuities.

Physically Seoul is a dramatic place:

bare, craggy mountains define the skyline to the north, the steep slopes of Mount Namsan climb right out of the city's central district, while the broad, slow waters of the Han River to the south divide the old city from the new Olympian developments on the other side.

Only a handful of years ago, Seoul was in a permanent state of chaos: everywhere one went the roads were up, and the traffic was manic. Now the sub-

Cherry blossom at Seoul's Kyongbok Palace.

way is complete and sanity has returned, and though the city continues to teem with people in a way that will astonish newcomers to the Orient, getting around is on the whole quick, easy and cheap. True, there is an art to catching a cab (know your destination, bellow it through the window, and don't feel unduly hurt if the driver declines to take you), and there are far too many intersections where pedestrians are forced to negotiate underpasses instead of being allowed to cross at lights. But on the plus side, Seoul is a far more compact and manageable city than it seems on that first long ride into town from the airport. Most of the interesting historical sites are walkable from the main hotels, or accessible by subway in a matter of minutes. The most important exception is It'aewon, home of the United States Eighth Army and location of most foreigner-oriented stores and night clubs, which is neither walkable nor close to the subway. But it's only fifteen-odd minutes by taxi.

Within this mountain-fringed, madly-teeming but manageable city, which has had a central place in the nation's history for nearly 600 years, an extraordinary variety of scenes and sensations await the visitor with even half an ounce of enterprise. The generous, serene gardens of Kyongbok Palace and the royal retreat at Piwon, the Secret Garden, are no great distance from the bargain blue jeans and populistic gourmandizing of the markets at the East and South Gates (Tongdaemun, Namdaemun). At Pagoda Park granddads nod over games of *Go*: hop in a cab and quick as a flash you can be dancing the night away in one of It'aewon's discos. In between you might catch the stately neo-classical architecture of Toksu Palace and its marvelous collection of modern Korean paintings, grab a few won's worth of *bondegi*, steaming silkworm cocoons boiled in soy sauce, or a dish of oya fish from a pavement stand, or make a luxurious evening

of it with a vast Korean banquet in the private room of a *kisaeng* house in Insa-dong.

Reminders of Korea's deep-seated problems are inescapable: the heights of the city's mountains still belong to the army, and the center is full of very young, very conspicuous plainclothes government security men. If you are here in May, when the university exams finish, you may be unlucky enough to catch a blast of tear gas wafting down from the city's campuses, where police will be breaking up yet another protest by students at the snail-like pace of the nation's progress toward democratic government. But equally, the rude vigor and confidence of the country are evident everywhere, too; the tall, aggressive new buildings sprouting on every block that have transformed the city's looks in the past decade, and the press of fashionable, prosperous youth through the streets of Myong-dong, where the boutiques and department stores are concentrated.

GETTING STARTED

Administratively speaking, Seoul is a "special city," with the same status as a province. The city is divided into 16 *gu* or wards, each of which is further divided into *dong* or precincts. Main roads are divided by length into *ka,* sections. However, knowing the exact address of where you want to go does not necessarily guarantee that you will find it. As new roads and buildings are superimposed on the city's essentially medieval layout, the streets and lanes of Seoul form an evermore complex maze, especially since all new construction must now be designed around the old palaces, shrines, city gates and so on which have been declared national monuments. To compound the problem, house numbers are not assigned in logical, sequential order but according to the date the house was built. So the best way to get around Seoul on your own is to memorize a few major landmarks and then work your way to specific destinations from there.

Probably the single most useful point for the visitor to orientate him or herself to is the main hotel district, with the Lotte and Chosun Hotels at its center. From here you are only a few steps away from City Hall, Toksu Palace and the bustling Myong-dong shopping and pleasure district (all described below). The single word "It'aewon" will be enough to get you to that vital part of town, reached through the tunnels that pierce Namsan (South Mountain). To reach the colorful markets of eastern Seoul, as well as Seoul Stadium and its mass of sporting goods shops, the key word is **Tongdaemun,** "Great East Gate."

For visitors in the city for a matter of days or weeks, taxis, subway and feet are certainly the best ways to get around. Taxis become a problem in the evening when everyone wants to ride them and there are simply not enough to go round, because (it is said) of the restriction on gasoline imports (Korea still has one of the world's largest foreign debts). Unless you shout your destination clearly as the cabs cruise past, you risk being left

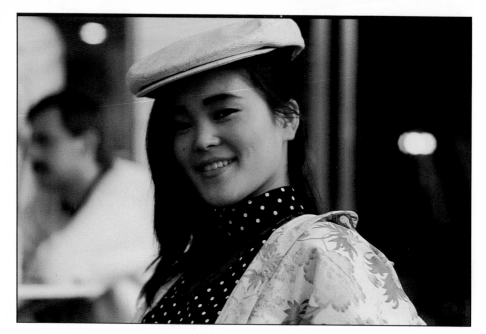

stranded by the side of the road for-ever. If several fares are going in the same direction the driver will take them all, though you will usually still have to pay the amount shown on the meter. Larger "call taxis" are more often available because their fares start at ₩1,000 instead of the normal ₩600. For wealthy you they are a sen-sible alternative to hanging about. You can either book them by special road-side phones or hail them if they are cruising.

If you stay in the city longer than a few weeks, or if you are taken around by a Korean friend, you may start rid-ing the buses. This is not recommended for solitary newcomers because desti-nations are only written in *han'gul*. To take a bus, first buy a token (₩120) at one of the many kiosk stores on the main streets - these are always found close to bus stops. Alternatively pay ₩130 in cash. In either case you pay as you enter. People waiting for buses in Seoul do not form lines but mill around in the general area then make a con-certed dash for the door when it arrives. Great fun.

CITY SIGHTS

The word Seoul means "capital," and its history as such begins in 1392 when King T'aejo established the Yi dynasty here, usurping the power of the Koryo dynasty which had been based in Kaesong, now a short way over the border in North Korea. It has remained the pre-eminent city ever since, though frequently threatened and more than once destroyed by invaders. The strongest reminders of how the city must have looked in the past are its gates: five of the original nine remain (though not all in their original loca-tions). Formerly they were linked by a ten-mile wall of earth and dressed stone which was the city's boundary, only fragments of which survive to-day, some on Pugak-san, the mountain on the city's north side, some on Nam-san, the mountain which is now close to the city's center. The modern city flows way beyond the area which the

The trendy lady in It'aewon, ABOVE, and the para-gon of traditional virtue, OPPOSITE, might just be the same person.

wall circumscribed.

For most of its existence Seoul has been a royal capital, and the most beautiful sights in the city, reserved for king and court in the past but now open to the public, allow vivid glimpses of the old royal lifestyle. The two places which no visitor should miss are **Kyongbok Palace,** "the Palace of Shining Happiness," and **Changdok Palace** with its **Secret Garden.**

Kyongbok Palace

Kyongbokkung was built in 1394 by King T'aejo and was the center of his government until the annexation of the country by the Japanese in 1910. Even then it did not lose its centrality, for the Japanese built the monumental domed **Capitol Building** directly in front of Kunjong-jon ("Hall of Government by Restraint"), where for centuries kings had received ministers and issued edicts. Both survive today, in the same uncomfortable proximity. The Capitol was a massive and remarkably unambiguous affront to the old regime, a frank declaration that the old ways had been superseded for good, and so it remains. The Capitol Building now functions as the National Museum, recently renovated, the greatest treasure-house in the country of relics from every stage of its history. Meanwhile the Blue House, the official residence of the country's present-day ruler from which he issues *his* edicts, is located just to the north of the palace.

The grounds of Kyongbok Palace spread elegantly for acres to the north of the Capitol Building and contain so much of interest that to appreciate them fully takes days. Some of the old palace buildings have been faithfully reconstructed, among them **Sujongjon, Hall of Talented Scholars,** where *han'gul*

was invented, and **Kyonghoeru, Hall of Happy Meetings,** an enormous open banquet pavilion set in the middle of an artificial lake, which is still occasionally used for entertaining foreign dignitaries. All convey a strong sense of the severity and love of order at the Yi dynasty's neo-Confucian heart. But the severity is mollified by love of nature, provided nature, too, is properly pruned and organized, and the gardens of Kyongbok are exquisite and serene, especially on days when there aren't

too many thousands of schoolchildren trooping around. The popular vote for the prettiest spot goes without question to the petite **Hyangwon Pavilion** in the north-east corner, set on a small, round island in a square pond bursting with pink flowering lotuses in summer, fringed by weeping willow, miniature maple and flowering lilac trees.

The grandest structure in the palace, over in the East, is a massive, **ten-story pagoda** dating from the Koryo kingdom, some six hundred years ago.

At the northernmost extreme, farthest away from the Capitol, is a **Folk Museum** which provides newcomers to Korea with a foretaste of what they will find when they set off into the countryside. The waxwork displays give a good idea of the traditional environments in which ordinary Koreans used to live and work, the clothes they

---

Age and youth. The elderly man with the sage-like features, ABOVE, is from the tradition-steeped environs of Andong.

wore and the food they ate. Here you can inspect the fabulous assortment of hats old Korea used to affect; learn how kimch'i is made and the sort of fuel used to fire the *ondol* (wood, rice straw, barley chaff - practically anything), and see samples of the movable type used by Korean printers way back in the thirteenth century.

Kyongbok was burned down by the Japanese during their invasion of 1592, rebuilt between 1865 and 1869, then destroyed again by the Japanese this century. Of the original 330 structures, only ten major buildings survive today. Next to the Folk Museum is a stele commemorating the place where, in 1895, a party of Japanese assassins attacked Queen Min, stabbing her, then burning her with kerosene. If Korean feelings about Japan remain cool to this day, Kyongbok suggests a number of reasons why.

Changdok Palace

Destroyed by Hideyoshi's invaders but restored several times since, Changdok is Seoul's best-preserved palace, and the last-surviving members of the old ruling family continue to live in a secluded corner of the grounds. Appropriately enough, nowhere in Seoul feels more pleasantly insulated from the modern world. The royal garage here still houses the king's old limousines, a 1903 Cadillac and a 1909 Daimler, as well as an odd royal conveyance, a compromise between a pallanquin and a rickshaw, with a single large wheel dead center. The residential buildings have a nested, intimate quality which contrasts with the formal pomp of the state rooms.

Behind the palace are the tranquil seventy-eight acres of the Secret Garden, ponds, woods, pavilions and shady groves, all linked by rustic paths. Here you will find the king's "**Humble Education Place**," **Yon-gyongdang** a modest villa where the king liked to retire to

do some creative role-playing, Marie Antoinette style, dressing, eating and passing the time like a simple, countrified gentleman-scholar.

Changdok and the Secret Garden deserve to be explored at leisure, but unfortunately this is not possible: the only way to see them is in a guided group. Conducted in English, Japanese, Chinese and Korean, tours leave the main entrance at fixed times every day (English language tours are at 11:30 am, 1:30 pm and 3:30 pm), and cover the ground at a brisk pace.

Toksu: The Palace of "Virtuous Longevity"

The **Toksu Palace,** which is the most accessible from the central hotel district, is just across from Seoul Plaza Hotel and City Hall. Toksugung's royal audience hall was built at about the same time as Peking's Forbidden City and shows strong Chinese influence. Behind are smaller residential buildings, and to one side the fine neoclassical **Museum of Modern Art,** built by a British architect at the turn of the century.

80

Smaller in scale than Kyongbok or Changdok, Toksu Palace can be explored in an hour or two. The gardens are a pretty sight, especially in spring when the famous peony garden draws thousands of visitors, and in the fall when the ginko trees are aflame. A statue of the great King Sejong presides over the garden the year round.

Chongmyo

The **Chongmyo Shrine** lies in a secluded garden southeast of Changdok Palace and houses the ancestral tablets of the Yi dynasty kings and their queens. Visitors are free to wander through the thickly wooded grounds, but the two courtyards and main shrine hall are usually kept closed except on certain ceremonial holidays.

One of these falls annually on the first Sunday in May, when a colorful Confucian ceremony is held there to honor the spirits of Korea's royal ancestors (see "Religion" in **The Culture of Korea**). If you are in Seoul on that day make an effort to see this traditional ceremony, during which celebrants dressed in traditional costume pay homage to the spirits with offerings of food and wine, and play exotic court music on reed-pipe flutes, stone chimes, heavy drums, wooden clappers and other ancient instruments.

A short way towards the center of town from the shrine, on Chongno Street, is the diminutive **Pagoda Park**, the place where the popular Independence Movement of 1919 got under way. Now it's a haven from the city's noise and fumes, especially for elderly men, who spend hours here when the weather is good playing *go* or reading the paper.

These are Seoul's most interesting royal sights. Other places in the city of compelling interest are:

Namsan and the Pugak Skyway

The mountain called **Namsan**, with its needle-tipped tower, is Seoul's most conspicuous landmark. Surrounding it is an expansive and beautifully landscaped park. The drive up around Namsan is especially nice in spring, when cherry blossoms, forsythia and azalea burst into bloom, and in the fall. Formerly closed to the public for security reasons, the tower is now open for sightseeing. The restaurant at the top of the tower offers marvelous views of the city.

Opposite Namsan is the **Pugak Skyway**, which runs along the crest of Seoul's northern hills. No pedestrian traffic is permitted on the skyway, so you'll have to visit it by private car, taxi or tour bus. At the top is **Sky House**, which has a bar and restaurant and provides sweeping views of Seoul. From there you can also see some of the remains of the old wall which used to protect the city from attack.

Chogye Temple

The only important temple in Seoul, **Chogye Temple** is headquarters of

---

ABOVE a pavilion in Piwon, the "Secret Garden" attached to Changdok Palace.

Korea's official Chogye sect of Buddhism and the administrative center of 1,500 affiliated temples throughout the country. Located in the central Insadong area, it is walkable from the central hotel district. Though always colorful and humming with pious activity, by far the best time to visit Chogye-sa (*sa* means "temple") is on Buddha's birthday, which falls on the eighth day of the fourth lunar month (usually early or mid-May). This auspicious event is celebrated with great fanfare at Chogye-sa and other Buddhist temples around the country. On the eve of the holiday the faithful purchase paper lanterns to which they attach long streamers inscribed with the names of their family members. Illuminated by little candles, these are hung by the hundred in the temple grounds, and as evening falls the worshipers chant prayers for a prosperous and peaceful year to come. Women dressed in billowy, pastel *hanbok* crowd the courtyards, adding color and cacophony to the scene, and the air fills with simultaneously conducted sutra-chanting and Western choral singing. Many foreign residents of Seoul participate in this annual celebration by purchasing and hanging paper lanterns of their own. Why not you? The cost, which is basically a contribution to the temple, runs to about ₩10,000.

Tongdaemun and Namdaemun

The Great East and Great South Gates are the two of Seoul's five ancient city gates which have survived to the present. These fine examples of traditional Korean architecture, pockmarked by shells from the Korean War, do not really require that you make a special trip to go and see them, but they are convenient landmarks for the city's two biggest and most fantastic markets, also called Tongdaemun and Namdaemun. For more about these, see the following section.

SHOPPING IN SEOUL

Seoul is one of the best places in the world for shopping, and many visitors come for no other reason. Whether it is traditional Korean products such as antique chests, celadon, silk and ginseng that appeal, or contemporary items such as clothes, calculators, watches and sports accessories, Seoul offers a wide range of high-quality products, often at ridiculously reasonable prices.

There are a number of major shopping districts in the city, and each tends to specialize in certain types of products.

These are Korea's most popular products, followed by a list of the best shopping districts:

Ginseng, Korea's first export, is available here in all its many forms: dried roots, liquid extract, powder, capsules, candied slices, instant tea, soap,

ABOVE Statue of nationalist hero Kim Ku in Seoul's Namsan Park. OPPOSITE the Capitol Building, constructed by the Japanese, behind Kwanghwa-mun Gate. OVERLEAF In Seoul the desolate, craggy mountains are never far away.

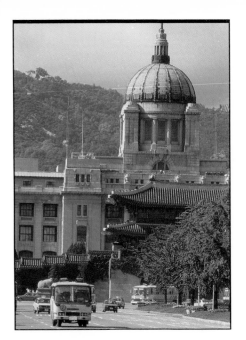

Market, where hard bargaining is the order of the day. Start your bidding low, roll your eyes in outrage at the counter-offer, raise your bid a bit, threaten to take your business elsewhere, and so forth, until you've struck a good bargain. For ready-made silk clothing, the boutiques of Myong-dong and the hotel arcades are good places to shop.

Korean Ceramics have been highly praised for centuries for quality of craftsmanship and originality of design. Celadon, with its distinctive blue-green glaze and white inlaid designs, is by far the most famous product of Korean kilns. Although all the best celadon was made more than 600 years ago, before the Yi dynasty, contemporary potters make excellent reproductions of this as well as of delicate white Yi dynasty porcelain and the earthy pots of the Shilla period with their characteristic perforated legs. The sort of items available include stemmed wine cups, long-necked wine decanters, tea-cups and tea pots, incense burners, vases and decorative bowls.

shampoo, skin cream and cigarettes. A box of fifty five-year-old roots of white ginseng currently retails for about $50 in Seoul. Red ginseng is more potent, more expensive and more difficult to find. Because ginseng is a state monopoly, prices are fixed nationwide, so have no qualms about buying ginseng at any place you happen to find it.

Silk is another famous Korean product that goes back a long way, and experienced fabric shoppers will quickly recognize the great silk bargains that are to be found in Seoul. Today, most American department stores buy their finished silk products wholesale in Korea, and even Thailand imports considerable quantities of raw silk to make its famous polished "Thai silk" products. Korean silk comes in an incredible variety of colors and patterns, both in prints and brocades, and it is suitable for clothing as well as decorative use. If the item you want is a mixture of silk and synthetics, it should be considerably cheaper than the pure silk equivalent.

Seoul's largest selection of silk in bulk is found in the **Tongdaemun**

The best-known and most accessible area to buy ceramics, antique chests and furniture is **Insa-dong**, near the center of town, but prices are steep, partly reflecting the high rents here. Much the cheapest and most interesting place to buy antique pots as well as chests, old silk clothing and other antiques is **Changan-dong**, a taxi ride out to the east of the city center. The first floors of two adjacent buildings are full of little antique shops, and as the goods overflow onto the street the buildings are easy to spot. Dealers will try to persuade you that their Shilla-style pots really are 1,500 years old, and that they are often believed is a tribute to the innocence of their customers. But there are plenty of bargains around for the discriminating.

New ceramics are available in every arcade and department store in Seoul, but be forewarned: blue-green celadon

is expensive everywhere in Korea because about ninety per cent of all production is destroyed owing to minor imperfections. This does ensure that the piece you buy will be perfect.

In It'aewon you'll find shops which sell original antiques as well as excellent reproductions at reasonable prices. While It'aewon does not have the best quality antiques in Seoul it certainly has the best prices, and for reproductions may well be the best place to shop. If you decide that you prefer the genuine article, remember that antiques of real value must be cleared for export with a certificate from the Cultural Properties Maintenance Office, and this can be a lengthy process. The office is in Seoul (tel: 731-61867) and has a branch office at Kimp'o Airport (tel: 662-0106). When buying what look like rare antiques, always be sure to check that the item is exportable.

For casual clothes and consumer products, Seoul is Mecca. In It'aewon you can buy the same shirts, sweaters, jackets and pants exported to and sold in American department stores for about one-third of the prices - and you can find closely similar items for even less on the stalls of Tongdaemun or Namdaemun markets, if you don't mind conducting your transactions in Korean. Watches, calculators, lighters and so forth are sold in arcades and department stores all over the city. For contemporary fashions, the boutiques of **Myong-dong** and hotel arcades offer quality clothing which in style is often only weeks behind the West, at much lower prices.

Other items to look for while shopping in Seoul include lacquerware inlaid with mother-of-pearl, brassware, embroidered Korean quilt covers, bedspreads and pillow-cases, bamboo and woven-straw products, amethyst and smoky topaz, leather and eelskin clothing and wood carvings.

Seoul's shopping districts are well-

organized and easy to find, although the sheer number of shops and products may bewilder. The best way to shop in Seoul is to select one or two districts per day and cover them thoroughly. Restaurants, snack stalls, coffee shops and beer halls are to be found in and around every shopping district. These are the principal ones:

Myong-dong: In the heart of downtown Seoul, only a block away from the Chosun and Lotte Hotels, Myong-dong is Seoul's busiest district and its center of high fashion, a maze of narrow lanes full of fashion boutiques, silk shops, shoe stores, and custom tailors as well as Korean, Japanese and Chinese restaurants, coffee-shops, *tabang* (tea well as stores specializing in Korean furniture, celadon and white porcelain, wood carving, scrolls and paintings, and beautifully embroidered Korean quilt covers, bedspreads and pillow-cases, both in silk and synthetics. Korean pillow-cases make especially nice gifts for friends back home because they are easy to carry, inexpensive and typically Korean in design. Insa-dong's antiques are both the highest quality and the highest-priced in the city. Among the most attractive antiques are herbal medicine cabinets, clothing chests, and antique dressing cases complete with mirrors and miniature drawers. In the side lanes of this interesting district are some of the city's most elegant traditional restaurants and *kisaeng* houses, including **Sanchon Vegetarian Restaurant** which has performances of traditional arts nightly. In these lanes you can also observe craftsmen at work in their street-side stalls.

Namdaemun Market: Within walking distance of the Chosun Hotel is the **"Great South Market,"** a colorful bazaar of open-air stalls selling local foodstuffs, contemporary clothing, bulk fabrics and miscellaneous household items. Wander through the fresh fish and vegetable markets for a first-hand look at Oriental grocery shopping. Dog meat, an Oriental delicacy prized for its tonifying effect [sic] on the vital organs, used to be sold in certain stalls here, but disappeared as the result of a government attempt to suppress the taste, and now you must go further afield to sample it. In Namdaemun you'll find good bargains in ready-made casual wear, souvenirs and various local knick-knacks. Always try to bargain for a better price in local markets like this. It's the accepted custom.

Tongdaemun Market: Near the an-

shops), "stand-bars," salons and beer-halls. Myong-dong bustles from morning till midnight. It's Seoul's equivalent of Ginza in Tokyo, Fifth Avenue in New York or Knightsbridge in London. Since Myong-dong's shops are geared towards the tastes and budgets of followers of high fashion, they tend to be a bit expensive. However, it's a great place to browse at any time, and meals at the little Korean restaurants there remain a bargain.

Insa-dong: Sometimes called **"Mary's Alley"** by foreigners, Insa-Dong is located not far from Chogye Temple, a short distance north of the Chosun and Lotte Hotels. The main street is lined with art galleries and antique shops as

Seoul is a market: fake "brand" goods, folk handicrafts and purely functional baskets and mats are among the million things for sale. Myong-dong TOP RIGHT is the most fashionable area to shop.

cient Great East Gate on Chongno Street, this is the biggest market in Korea. Spread over ten city blocks, the "Great East Gate Market" is divided into a number of buildings, each of which specializes in different types of products.

The main building, six stories high and two blocks long, is where you'll find the best bargains in Korean silk and synthetic brocades. Row upon row of little stalls, their bolts of fabric spilling colorfully into the aisles, vie for the attention of passing shoppers. Here you can purchase traditional *hanbok* costumes ready-made, for men and women, silk fabric in bulk, buttons, zippers, pendants and other tailoring accessories, embroidered quilt-covers, bedspreads, pillow-cases and attractive floorcushions. With a bit of bargaining you can really obtain some good buys in this sprawling market-place. Of course it is always best to take along a Korean acquaintance to a place like this, but basic English, the few vital questions listed in **Travelers' Tips** and sign language will be enough to see you through.

The other side of the elevated highway from the main market hall is another massive building which specializes in ready-made casual wear, shoes, sandals and sundry household items. The shops in the vicinity of the nearby Seoul Stadium sell every conceivable variety of sports clothing and athletic equipment at bargain prices. There are other shopping arcades both above and below ground. It's a vast emporium.

It'aewon: Ever since the Japanese invasions of 1592-98, during which many Japanese soldiers married Korean women and settled down here, It'aewon has been Seoul's major foreign enclave. Today it is a lively avenue of clothing shops, tailors, restaurants, coffee-shops, bars and night clubs, all of which are geared toward the tastes and budgets of American GIs stationed at Yongsan.

For export-quality contemporary cloth-

ing, It'aewon is the best place in Seoul to shop. Such stores as Muriel's Sweater Shop offer the latest in sports shirts, blouses, sweaters and other garments at remarkably low prices. Jackets, belts, bags, wallets, shoes and other leather and eelskin items are good value here. There are also shops which specialize in brassware, lacquerware, antique reproductions and souvenirs. Almost all proprietors in It'aewon speak sufficiently good English to conduct business with foreign customers.

An interesting local open-air market runs parallel to the south side of the main street, in a long alley just behind the clothing shops and tailors. Here you'll find local produce, cooking utensils and household items for sale, as well as little eateries specializing in various types of Korean snack food.

Department Stores: Seoul's major department stores are as big and modern as anything in the West, and they should definitely be included on any serious shopper's itinerary. Located in and around Myong-dong, they offer at fixed prices the whole range of consumer products manufactured in Korea.

The biggest of them is the **Lotte Shopping Center,** next door to the Lotte Hotel. Start your browsing in the basement of the food department, where the array of Korean and Western culinary products is incredible. Bakery items are especially good. The next seven floors are devoted to the usual sort of products stocked by department stores everywhere. The eighth floor is entirely given over to a duty-free shop for tourists, and is divided into a section for Korean products and one for brand-name luxury items imported from abroad. The ninth and tenth floors have been dubbed "Food Street," and accommodate two dozen restaurants offering everything from oriental to western cuisine and from snacks to feasts.

These are the names, addresses, phone numbers and official weekly holidays of Seoul's major department stores:

Lotte Shopping Center, 1 Sokong-dong, Chung-gu. Tel: 771-25 (Tuesday).

Midopa Department Store, 123, 2-ka, Namdaemun-ro, Chung-gu. Tel: 754-2222 (no holiday).
Shinsegae Department Store, 51-2, 1-ka, Chungmu-ro, Chung-gu. Tel: 754-1234 (Monday).
Cheil Department Store, 31-1, 2-ka Myong-dong, Chung-gu. Tel: 776-2741 (Thursday).
Cosmos Department Store, 83-5, 2-ka Myong-dong, Chung-gu. Tel: 776-2601 (Tuesday).

Shopping Arcades: Seoul's shopping arcades are among the most extensive in Asia. Major downtown hotels such as the Chosun, Lotte and Seoul Plaza each have their own arcades of shops, which sell everything from celadon, silk and ginseng to cameras, watches, cosmetics and Western fashions. Despite the expensive ambiance, the prices as well as the quality of many items are broadly comparable with those sold in the department stores and other arcades.

Many of the underground passageways used by pedestrians to cross Seoul's main streets serve as vast shopping arcades, especially in the downtown area. Seoul's major shopping arcades are:

Underground:
Bando Chosun (below the Chosun Hotel).
Lotte First Avenue (below Lotte Hotel and Shopping Center).
Sokong (adjacent to Bando Chosun Arcade).
Ulchi (beneath Ulchi Road, 2-ka).
Chonggak (beneath Chongno Road, 2-ka).
Haehyon (beneath Namdaemun Road, near Great East Gate).

Above ground:
Seun (along Chongno Road, 4-ka).
Sampung (along Ulchi Road, 4-ka).
Tongbang Building Arcade.
Daewoo Building Arcade.

Yol (mattresses) and *ibol* (bedspreads) in lurid abundance at a store in Tongdaemun.

Duty-Free Shops: Seoul has a number of special duty-free shops and Foreign Commissaries exclusively for the use of foreign shoppers. The former sell Western luxury items and liquor as well as local handicrafts. You can use either local or foreign currencies, but you must show your passport. Duty-free shops are located at **Kimp'o International Airport,** the **Lotte Shopping Center, eighth floor,** the **Nam Moon Shop** (5 Yang-dong, Chung-ku), **Ungchon Company** (15 Insa-dong, Chongro-gu), the **Dong-wha Shop** (1- 41 Sajik-dong, Chongro-ku), **Hotels Shilla, Hanjin** (at Seoul Station) and **Diamond** (at Mugyo-dong). Foreign Commissaries stock common American foods such as peanut butter, cheese-spread, potato chips, etcetera, as well as toiletries and other items. Both tourists and foreign residents may shop in these commissaries, which are located in the Chosun Hotel arcade, the Lotte basement arcade, Myong-dong, and elsewhere about town.

SEOUL BY NIGHT

Seoul is an industrious city, but by no means a puritanical one. When the working day is done Koreans put their work ethics away in their briefcases, loosen their ties and go mad. You can go mad, too, and stay that way as long as you like.

It wasn't always thus. Until 1981 a strictly imposed midnight curfew lent a quality of desperation to the city's night life, especially toward 11:30 pm, when revelers poured their drinks down their throats, rushed about in a last-minute search for companions, then scrambled back to homes or hotels before the witching hour struck. Since it has been lifted, however, the nervous tension has happily dissipated, and today Seoul can boast one of Asia's most colorful and varied night scenes, with something for every taste and budget.

Whether you are seeking Western- or Korean-style entertainment, a modern or traditional ambiance, low-budget beer halls and tea- rooms or high-rolling nightclubs and casinos, Seoul has them all. For the reader's convenience, this section is divided into two parts, Western-style and Korean-style. Bear in mind that whatever you find in Seoul after dark will have its equivalents elsewhere in the country; once you've mastered the scene here, other cities are a breeze.

Western Style

If you like to begin the evening with cocktails, the bars of the leading hotels will get you off to the best start. The most enduringly popular is the **Ninth Gate Bar** in the lobby of the Westin Chosun Hotel, which has good live music. Another popular spot is the painfully named **Bobby London Pub** in the lower arcade of the Lotte Hotel. Alternatively try the **Banjul,** which also has live music and a good Western restaurant and hostess club on its upper floors. The Banjul is located two lanes behind the Samilro Building. Single men might like to start the evening with a few drinks at the **Tiger House,** diagonally opposite the Chosun Hotel, or at the Savoy Hotel's **Goody-Goody Bar,** located in the basement.

Seoul's history as a cosmopolitan city only goes back a few years, and the most reliable places to eat good European and American food are still the international hotels. Each of Seoul's leading deluxe hotels has at least one good gourmet restaurant featuring Western cuisine, and though prices tend to be high, the culinary standards and the service may be said to justify it. Seoul's first gourmet French restaurant was the Chosun's **Ninth Gate,** and it still re-

OPPOSITE Bridges over Seoul's Han River at dusk.

mains in favor. Its decor strikes a good balance between opulence and restraint, and the menu offers traditional favorites as well as innovative house specialties.

Of the 31 restaurants and bars operated by the Lotte Hotel, the **Prince Eugene** provides the most splendid luxury. Its palatial decor is matched by one of the most impressive menus in town – and some of the highest prices. For a more subdued ambiance try the Hyatt Regency's **Hugo's Restaurant,** a fine continental restaurant with a well-founded reputation, or perhaps the **Celadon Restaurant** on the second floor of the Sheraton Walker Hill, where the food is complemented by celadon and German crystal. Buffet enthusiasts will find Seoul's most bountiful buffet table, groaning with Western as well as Japanese and Korean selections, at the Shilla Hotel's **Shangri-la Restaurant,** built into a wing of the old Yi dynasty guest-house there. If you fancy a steak

cooked the American way, try the **El Toro** on the second floor of the Seoul Plaza Hotel.

If you wish to escape from the hotels and their prices, there are a few places on the outside which serve good Western food in pleasant surroundings. **La Cantina** (tel: 771-2579), located directly across from the Lotte Hotel in the basement of the Sam Sung Building, serves authentic Italian cuisine at reasonable prices and is quite popular with Seoul's resident foreign community. Or maybe you would like to rub shoulders with Korea's most popular entertainers, many of whom dine Western-style at the **Hee Joon** (tel: 265-1466), a cozy dinner club with live music in the basement of the Kuk-dong Building.

What next? How about a show? Seoul has a number of interesting theater-restaurants, which feature excellent entertainment but only mediocre cooking. The best idea is to eat elsewhere and arrive in time for the show, which usually begins around 8 pm. The **Kayagum Theater Restaurant** at the Sheraton Walker Hill stages the most extravagant floor shows in town. The

ABOVE A hint of Paris in It'aewon, Seoul's most international section, which is slowly becoming more up-market.

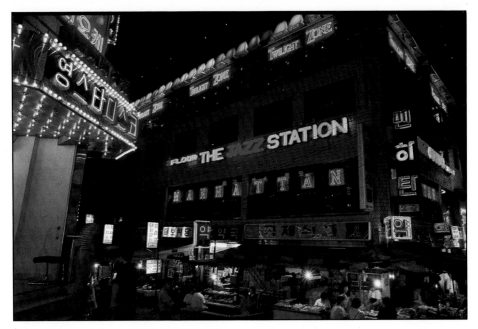

night begins with a thoroughly vulgarized presentation of traditional Korean music and dance, but after the horsehair hatted band calls it quits, looking understandably grumpy, the real fun begins. The Western part of the show - truly Western, almost all the performers being either European or American - is elaborately staged and slickly enjoyable for anyone who has been away from this sort of thing for a time. It's topless but harmless, so don't feel shy about going *à deux*.

The Sheraton Walker Hill also has the only casino in Seoul, one of the eleven in the country, each located at a different tourist center. Only non-Koreans are allowed to gamble at these casinos.

Connoisseurs of classical music should try to catch a concert, opera or symphony while in Seoul. The standards are high, and a number of Korean musicians have attained international fame. The **Sejong Cultural Center**, located opposite the American Embassy on Sejong Road, and the **National Theater**, home of Korea's National Ballet, National Symphony and National Opera, both stage regular performances featuring well-known Korean as well as international musicians, singers and dancers. For current programs and schedules call the Korean Culture and Arts Foundation (tel: 741-0051)

If you prefer pop music, the best place in central Seoul may well be **OB's Cabin** (tel: 776-4784), a four-floor music club popular with Seoul's foreign community. It's in the heart of Myong-dong, two lanes behind UNESCO House. **All that Jazz** (tel: 792-5701), at 168-17 It'aewon-dong, is Seoul's best jazz club, with American disc-jockeys and live jam sessions three times a week.

Most of Seoul's big hotels have discotheques. The Lotte's **Annabelle's**, the Chosun's **Club Tomorrow** and the Shilla's **Club Universe** are all very popular, as are the discos at the Hyatt and Sheraton Walker Hill. Another good dancing club is the **Club Copa-**

ABOVE It'aewon at night. Discos upstairs, stalls selling snacks on the street below.

93

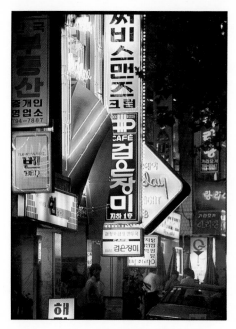

wears on. **All that Jazz**, mentioned above, is across the road and a little way down the hill from the Sportsman's. The steep, narrow lane behind the Sportsman's, known variously as GI Alley or the Village, is lined with bars and clubs of various shapes and sizes where the mixture of country-and-western music, paunchy, aging

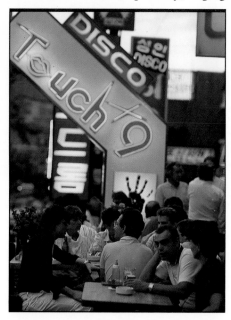

cabana (tel: 777-2947), located in a narrow lane behind Tiffany's, with two floors of dancing and American DJs. Seoul's disco clubs are equally enjoyable for couples and for singles, and unattached guests usually have no problem finding partners.

It'aewon, however, is much the best and most interesting place to dance in Seoul. There are several discos along the main road; entrance is usually free, drinks are cheaper than in the big hotels, and the It'aewon atmosphere is unique if a little weird. Most of the foreigners are male and military, while most of the girls are lithe young locals eager for a brush with the big world and happy to dance all night in exchange for a few beers. The best-known place is the **Sportsman's Club**, though others such as the **UN Tourist Club**, **King Club** and **Servicemen's Club** also warm up as the evening

military men and young Korean hostesses showing off their incredible legs in hot pants is piquant to say the least. Presence of mind is useful when moseying around in this part of town as daydreamers are liable to get yanked clean off the street by hookers not known for their subtlety. If you do sit down with a hostess in one of these clubs, you will naturally be expected to replenish her glass of colored water (and your own of whiskey or beer) at frequent intervals, but prices are reasonable by international standards. Beware, however, of catching something you can't get rid of. Be prepared.

Korean Style

Koreans, too, like to start a night on the town with a few quiet drinks, and in

Night scenes in It'aewon. ABOVE LEFT and OP-POSITE LEFT a few graphic arguments for learning to read Han'gul. ABOVE RIGHT It'aewon's foreigners are mostly though not exclusively military. OP-POSITE RIGHT Night scene at Lotte's open-air restaurant, central Seoul.

Seoul there is no shortage of places to sample. Myong-dong and other districts of downtown Seoul are full of Korean taverns and restaurants, and most of them can easily be identified by sight. Starting with the simplest, you could try a small bottle of *soju*, the sweet potato distillation which is the favorite of serious Korean drinkers, at one of the local bars, small, noisy, smoke-filled taverns where ruddy-faced workers exchange boisterous toasts while snacking on excellent *anju*. *Chogae* (clams grilled on the half-shell) and *sogum-gui* (grilled beef) are enduring *anju* favorites. Even simpler than such places are the *pojang-macha*, tent wagons with red, white and blue awnings located in alleys and byways all over Seoul. The

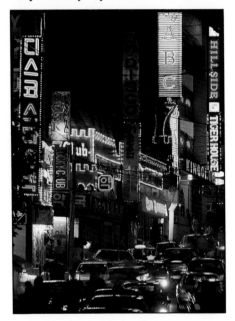

one that often comes to rest in the alley next to the Samilro Building can be recommended.

A step up from *soju* is *makkolli*, a cloudy rice brew which was traditionally Korea's most popular drink. **Tae Ryon** (tel: 265-5439) and **Chonggey-Oke** (tel: 267-2744), both located across the street from the Samilro Building, are typical *makkolli* houses

which serve particularly tasty *anju*. Behind the new high-rises at the Kwang-hwamun intersection, each with a blue "Jinro Limited" sign over the door, stand four *makkolli* houses in a row, where you can drink *yakchu* (highly-refined *makkolli*) and sample the excellent *pindaetok* (shrimp-studded, mung bean pancakes) and *chogaetang* (clam soup).

For foreigners, the most popular type of Korean drinking establishment seems to be the beer-hall, where chilled draft beer (*saeng maekju*), usually "OB" brand, and simple snacks are served. Small and cozy, beer-halls can grow quite lively. They are easily identified by square red signs with a frothy mug of beer inside a white ring. **Blue Villa** (tel: 23-3694) is one of numerous beer-halls located within a single block behind the Seoul Plaza Hotel in the direction of South Gate. There are plenty in Myong-dong, too - just keep walking until you come across one that strikes your fancy.

Another modern sort of Korean bistro is the "stand bar," where customers sit at a long bar while hostesses serve

them beer or whiskey and *anju,* and sometimes sit and chat. Stand-bars are especially popular with office workers, who head there after work to unwind. You'll find them all over Myong-dong and elsewhere around Seoul and they are usually identified as such in English.

By the time you leave your typical Korean *sul-jip* (liquor house), you should be ready for a hearty meal at a typical Korean *sik-tang* (restaurant).

One restaurant which stands out from the crowd and is likely to make dining Korean-style a treasured memory is **Dai Won Gak** (tel: 762-0161). It is set in a beautiful walled garden compound with individual dining pavilions, thatched cottages, landscaped ponds and waterfalls all connected by wooden walkways. The rustic setting and superb service are matched by the cuisine.

Korean restaurants in town range from little hole-in-the-wall eateries specializing in a single dish to elaborate, multi-storied food palaces with a widely-varied menu. The former certainly provide the most authentically Korean atmosphere. Whichever you choose, you will find that English is not generally understood, and that the menu will usually be written only in *han'gul.* The easiest and most agreeable way out of this dilemma is to take/be taken along by a Korean friend. Or take along the list of dishes printed in *han'gul* and English in the **Travelers' Tips** section of this book and study it with your waiter until you agree on a dish which he can produce and you can eat. Or cast an eye round at what the assembled diners are already eating and point boldly to one which looks all right. The rashest way is to pick out something at random from the illegible menu. Much safer to say, *"Araso chuseyo!"* - "I leave the choice to your discretion."

There are many *sik-tang* in Seoul, as in every town and village in the land.

But should you wish to splurge a bit, Seoul's gourmet scene will not disappoint you either.

Barbecued beef is at the heart of gourmet Korean cuisine, and good Korean beef-houses abound throughout Seoul. Try the **Buil Barbecued Rib House** (tel: 777-1666), located on Ulchi Road, or the famous **Han Il Kwan** (tel: 72-3077), a well-established chain with a high reputation, which has branches in Myong-dong and Chong-ro. Simply walk in, sit down and say *"Bulgogi"* or *"Kalbi,"* and everything will be taken

care of.

Besides beef, Korean restaurants are also justly famous for their seafood, noodles and chicken. The **Hamhung Naengymon,** across from the UNESCO House in Myong-dong, is one of Seoul's most famous buckwheat noodle houses. Korean chicken stuffed with rice, ginseng root and dried jujubes was described in **Korean Cuisine** (p. 58-64). Regarded as both a food and a medicine, this dish is as delicious as it is fortifying. Try it at the **Paekche Ginseng Chicken Restaurant** located in a

OPPOSITE Cabaret star at night club in Chungmuro, Seoul. ABOVE Dinner show at the Sheraton Walker Hill's Kayagum Theater Restaurant.

narrow passageway just behind the Commercial Bank of Korea off Myong-dong's main drag. Accompanied by a few shots of Jinro Ginseng Wine and topped off with a glass of fresh squeezed ginseng juice, this meal is a marvelous example of the great Far Eastern tradition of blending food and medicine.

Of course it is possible to sample the full range of Korean cuisine at the fancy (and rather expensive) restaurants in the major hotels. The Shilla's **Sorabol** and the Lotte's **Mugunghwa** serve traditional Korean fare in elegant surroundings, and English menus are available. At **Po Suk Jung** on floor B1 of the Lotte Hotel, the traditional meal is accompanied by a pocket-sized but skillful display of Korean dancing and music. Or you could opt for an evening at Korea House (see below), where the program of dancing and drama may be preceded by dinner either buffet-style or around a low lacquered table.

The ultimate dining experience in Seoul – one which combines traditional food, drink and entertainment within the context of classical Korean culture – is an evening at a *kisaeng* house, an experience which requires a considerable outlay of cash. Comparable in style and content to Japan's geisha houses, though less formal, the *kisaeng* house experience gives a fair idea of what it must have been like to be a moneyed aristocrat in the old days. The cost usually comes to about US$50-70 per person for food and drinks, plus another $30 or so in tips for the ladies who accompany guests throughout dinner, so count on spending about $100 per head.

Unless you happen to speak fluent Korean it's always advisable to visit a *kisaeng* house in the company of at least one Korean friend, otherwise you'll miss most of the fun. Your party will have its own private dining-room decorated in classical Korean fashion, and you will be served by a bevy of at-tractive young *kisaeng* clad in colorful Korean dress, who will pour your drinks, wipe your brow and generally keep you amused.

If you happen to establish a rapport with one of the girls during the evening, you may feel free to ask her out; she is under no obligation to accept, and if she does, her fee is bound to be high. Your Korean friend will act as intermediary, and he in turn will consult the house's *mama-san,* who makes all decisions and sets all the fees. On the other hand, if you are with a mixed group, don't hesitate to bring your own spouse or date to a *kisaeng* house; they're quite as happy to welcome mixed parties as all-male groups.

Seoul's most renowned and exclusive *kisaeng* house is **Sam Cheong Gak** (tel: 762-0151/59), a beautiful walled garden compound with a palatial banqueting hall and pavilions in a landscaped garden setting.

Accustomed to hosting foreign parties, the Sam Cheong Gak can handle groups of a hundred or more with equal ease. Another popular *kisaeng* house is the **Jang Won** (tel: 72-8645), located about 65 meters in front of the police box behind the US Embassy.

For a more contemporary though only slightly less expensive version of the *kisaeng* house, try a contemporary Korean salon. The service is essentially the same, but the setting is modern: tables and chairs instead of *ondol* floors, hostesses in gowns instead of *hanbok*. Salons abound in Seoul, and are easily identified by the word "salon" in English over the door.

The most extraordinary relic of Seoul's traditional night-life scene, one which will perhaps be lucky to survive the preparations for the Olympics but

OPPOSITE TOP The Korean show at the Sheraton Walker Hill makes up in spectacle for what it lacks in authenticity. The fan dance at Korea House BOTTOM relates more closely to the real thing.

which at the time of going to press was still flourishing, is the street of open-fronted brothels known universally in Seoul as **Miari Texas**. Miari is the name of the district; "Texas" has become the usual Korean euphemism for a red-light district (Pusan has one too), but apart from the name there is nothing remotely Texan about Miari Texas: a long row of blindingly brightly-lit stalls, hidden from the road by a line of trees, where extravagantly made-up women in gaudy *hanbok* sit and preen themselves and try to lure the strolling, gawking groups of businessmen inside. There is no charge for looking, and it's unlikely that you'll have the courage to do anything more anyway, but it's quite a spectacle. Miari Texas is in the north

Climax of the Korea House fan dance ABOVE and BELOW drummers galore at the Sheraton.

of the city, the other side of Pugak-san mountain. The simplest way to get there is by taxi, and the busiest and hence most interesting time to go is around 6 pm.

Back in the mainstream, and with your belly full of food, you may like to do the typically Korean thing and enjoy a few drinks after dinner at one of the many bars and tea shops that provide live music. At the **Sansoo Gapsan** (tel: 777-3125), located about ninety meters behind Tiffany, you'll find Seoul's best "classical music beerhall", where the punters are serenaded by string quartets and soloists. Musical coffee-shops and *tabang* (tea rooms) can usually be identified by the English word "music" or a sign with a few notes of music dancing next to a coffeecup. Usually located in the basement or second-floor of office buildings, they are as common in Seoul as cafes in Paris. A good example is the **Shim Won** (tel: 777-4781), located on the second floor of the building in the alley next to Unesco Building in Myongdong. In this alley, leading to the Savoy Hotel, there are numerous *tablangs,* all frequented by young people who like pop music. **Kamu** (tel: 776-3141); **Champion** (tel: 777-0988) and **Nulbom** (tel: 776-3391) are a few examples. For a quieter ambiance and classical music, try **June** (tel: 776-4447) or the **Phil Harmony** (tel: 776-4987), both located directly across the street from the Savoy Hotel.

Shows and Concerts

For an introduction to traditional music and dance, the government-sponsored **Korea House**, near the northern slopes of Namsan, is hard to beat. Set in an attractive garden, the traditionally-styled center has a nightly program of stage entertainment which includes shaman rituals, mask-dance drama and solos on classical instruments. In addition, free performances of folk dancing are given every Saturday and Sunday at 3 pm. There is a library of films which can be viewed on request, and a bookstand with a good selection of English-language publications about Korea. A restaurant serves traditional cuisine, and you may opt to eat either buffet-style in a dining-room with tables and chairs, or cross-legged in a private *ondol* room, served by waitresses in *hanbok*. The phone numbers of Korea House are 266-9101/4 and 267-8752.

The Sejong Cultural Center, mentioned above, right in the heart of the city and within view of the Capitol Building, was completed in 1978 and represents an early, groping attempt to find an architectural style that is both modern and Korean. The resulting slightly fascist look is a pity. The large hall has a ninety-nine-rank organ and performances of symphonies, plays and other works are frequently given. Along with the National Theater, this is one of the city's most important venues for top artists, both Korean and non- Korean.

TRADITIONAL INNS (*YOGWAN*)

For a stay at one of the few *yogwan* which retain the atmosphere of an earlier age, try the **Un Dang Yogwan**. A short way south of Changdok Palace and tricky to find unaided, it is buried away in one of the few central sections of town which has yet to feel the dead hand of development. Un Dang Yogwan (tel: 765-4194/7) was formerly the house of a nobleman, and the organiza-

tion of its many discrete parts, folded in on each other like an oversize game of dominoes, reflects that history. Raised above the ground on large stones, the larger pavilions originally accommodated the wealthy owner and his immediate family, while the smaller rooms to the side were reserved for retainers, parasites and poets. All are now part of the *yogwan*, and whichever you choose it is guaranteed to delight: the demerara-colored floors, the delicate woodwork and hand-made translucent paper, the surprising little gardens at every turn, the sumptuous traditional breakfast, and above all the uncanny tranquility of the place, all combine to make this unlike any other accommodation in the world. The Un Dang is not Seoul's most convenient accommodation, and can be far from tranquil at night when some of the guests have a party. Bathrooms are communal and the only air-conditioning is an electric fan. But few inns anywhere in the country offer a comparably rich experience of the traditional way of life.

In the narrow streets behind the Sejong Center are some of the *yogwan* which are most popular with young foreign travelers, as well as a number of good, moderately-priced restaurants. The two best-known *yogwan* are **Inn Daewon** (tel: 735- 7891) and **Inn Daeji** (tel: 737-4659). These are good places to stay if you are desperate for company and chat, or want to exchange information about traveling cheaply elsewhere in the country.

THE GRAND HOTELS

Like the rest of the country, Seoul has no shortage of accommodation, though for a crucial couple of weeks in 1988 that statement may be open to question. There are hotels and inns to suit every pocket and predilection, from simple inns and the traditional *yogwan* described on page 102, through efficient if flavorless concrete boxes and the gloomily genteel YMCA, to the five-star international hotels. Of the latter there are seven, and as much of the city's social life, for Western residents as well as visitors, continues to revolve around

them, here are profiles of each. A list of other, less expensive hotels in Seoul and elsewhere is provided in **Travelers' Tips**.

Westin Chosun

Seoul's most famous international hotel, the Chosun, opened its doors for business a full decade before its competitors, and since then has established an excellent reputation both with travelers and locally resident businessmen. If you are the type who prefers a quiet hotel with personal service and a somewhat old-fashioned atmosphere, choose the Chosun.

Among the Chosun's facilities are an outdoor swimming-pool, a rooftop buffet restaurant with fine views and a night club. But its most popular attraction is the **Ninth Gate Bar and Restaurant,** favorite international rendezvous. The bar's plate-glass windows look out on another unique Chosun feature, an old Yi dynasty pavilion, a registered national treasure, set in the midst of the Chosun's garden. Next to the bar is the Ninth Gate Restaurant, Seoul's first gourmet French restaurant and still one of the best.

The **Chosun** is located right in the center of the city, with convenient access by foot to major business, government and shopping centers. Most guests are FITs, foreign individual travelers, rather than tour groups, so even when the hotel is full it rarely seems crowded or noisy. Average room rates run at about $110 a night, while suites are between $275 and $800.

Lotte

With close on 1,000 rooms, the Lotte is Seoul's largest hotel: It has an enormous marble lobby, and a lobby lounge serving coffee and cocktails which looks out on a spectacular artificial waterfall. The Lotte's **Peninsula Coffee Shop** does a terrific and very popular buffet breakfast.

OPPOSITE The towers of the Lotte Hotel, set off by a Yi dynasty pavilion which belongs to neighboring Westin Chosun Hotel. ABOVE Dinner show in Lotte Hotel's Po Suk Jung Restaurant.

The Lotte is a fully computerized hotel geared to the needs of businessmen and large tour groups. With thirty-one restaurants and bars and a vast shopping arcade downstairs, it offers great variety in shopping and dining. It also has a health club and an indoor swimming pool. The hotel's sheer size, however, precludes the sort of personal attention and human warmth of a hotel like the Chosun. The Lotte is most appropriate for businessmen in a hurry and tour groups and conventions, but less appealing for individuals on holiday.

Located directly behind the Chosun, the thirty-eight-story Lotte is also in the city center and conveniently close to major businesses, government offices and shops. It has a wide range of rooms and rates, with average prices slightly below those at the Chosun.

Seoul Plaza

The third major hotel in the heart of town, the Seoul Plaza is only a stone's throw from the Chosun and Lotte. Rates in this 540-room hotel are slightly less than at the Chosun or Lotte, but the rooms are also smaller and the facilities less varied. The Plaza's greatest attractions are its five-star rating, which ensures good service and

professional management, and its location downtown. Guests of the hotel thus have easy access to the bars, restaurants and shops of the Chosun and Lotte hotels next door.

Shilla

Set on a hill at the foot of Mt Namsan, the tall, slender, 672-room Shilla opened for business in 1979, at the same time as the Lotte. Attached to it is an old Yi dynasty guest house which is still used for diplomatic receptions. Though pleasantly isolated from the noise and crowds of downtown, the Shilla is only fifteen minutes away from the city center by cab or hotel shuttle.

The Shilla's facilities include a health club, swimming pool, sauna and massage, disco and night club, and an elegant restaurant called the **Shangri-la** built into a wing of the old guest house, which does one of the best buffets in town. Because of its peaceful setting the Shilla has much to offer vacationing couples and families, but businessmen may find it too remote from the center of town, and single travelers may prefer a livelier setting.

The Shilla's greatest attraction is its twenty-three acre garden enclosed by a Shilla-style wall and reserved for the use of hotel guests. The garden has been planted with pine, juniper, red maple and flowering fruit trees, which makes it a pleasant retreat in all seasons. A jogging course winds its way up and down the shady slopes, so for dedicated joggers the Shilla is probably the best place to stay.

Rates at the Shilla average about $110 a night for a double room.

Hyatt Regency

From its perch on Mt Namsan, the glass-mirrored Hyatt has great panoramic views over the city. It is located about the same distance from downtown as the Shilla, though only a pre-

ABOVE Breakfast in Lotte Hotel's Peninsula Café.
OPPOSITE Seoul's Hyatt Hotel, which looms over It'aewon.

cipitous drop away from It'aewon. Among its many facilities are a large outdoor pool, a health club, a disco and a branch of **Hugo's**, Hyatt's restaurant chain.

The hotel is organized along standard Hyatt lines, which means the rooms are rather smaller than elsewhere and the atmosphere less distinctive. Frequent international travelers, however, may find the Hyatt attractive on account of the many conveniences this large international chain can provide. Rates are about the same as at the Shilla.

Sheraton Walker Hill

This is the most secluded of Seoul's major hotels as it is a good twenty minutes' drive from the center of town, in the midst of elaborately landscaped grounds. It is a large hotel, with 770 rooms and many recreational facilities, including indoor and outdoor pools, jogging and hiking trails, tennis courts, a nightclub and numerous restaurants.

The **Sheraton** has two major claims to fame: its theater-restaurant (see **Seoul By Night** for details) and its casino, the only one in Seoul. Due to its distance from downtown, the Sheraton's rates are the lowest of the major hotels, ranging from $70 to $115 a double room.

Seoul Hilton

The newest of the major hotels, the Seoul Hilton is located near the Great South Gate on the lower slopes of Mt Namsan and opened in 1983. The 629-room hotel has a fantastic lobby and Korean touches to the decor of the rooms. Facilities include an indoor swimming pool, an athletic club, top-floor executive suites with concierge, and a number of first-class restaurants. The center of town is about five minutes away by taxi. Room rates average about $95 a night.

SEOUL AREA SIDE-TRIPS

There is so much to see and do in Seoul that it is hard to drag oneself away, but the effort should be made. Even if you lack the time to travel further afield, there are a number of places close to the capital which can add quite a new dimension to your experience of the country. Each of the destinations described below may be visited from Seoul in the space of a day, though one or two merit an overnight stay if you can spare the time.

Korea is arguably one of the easiest countries in the world to travel around in. Tours are available to some of the best-known destinations - and the *only* way to see P'anmunjom in the Demilitarized Zone is on an official tour - but the traveler who treasures his freedom will be glad to know that in Korea independent travel is a piece of cake. Buses go everywhere, with unbelievable frequency (and sometimes great videos en route, too; *Dracula versus Billy the Kid* was one recent offering). Trains are dependable and comfortable. Highways are new and swift and remarkably under-used due to the high price of gas, and while a rented car is much the most expensive way to see the country, it may be the best if you're in a tearing hurry.

KOREAN FOLK VILLAGE

Perhaps you've already seen the waxworks of traditional Koreans in reconstructed environments inside the Folk Museum at Kyongbok Palace. **The Korean Folk Village** at Suwon, 51 km (32 miles) south of Seoul, takes the visitor an important step closer to understanding how traditional, rural Korea looked, smelled and tasted, the sort of spaces it felt at home in, where it locked up its criminals, and what it liked to do on its day off.

SEOUL ENVIRONS

To P'anmunjom
To Sanjong Lake Resort
Ch'unch'on
Imjung River
Kanghwa
Uijongbu
Namisom
Kanghwa-do
Ch'ongp'yong Resort
Kwangnung
Pukhansansong
Kumgok
Mt Yongmun
Chongdung-sa (temple)
Han River
Tonggu-Rung
SEOUL
Kimp'o
Int'l Airport
Namhansansong
Namhan River
Inch'on
Songnam
Songdo Resort
Kwangju
Shilluk-sa (temple)
Kyongbu Expressway
Suwon
Ich'on
Yongdong
Expressway
Korean Folk Village
Sohae
(West Sea)
N
10km
KYONGGI-DO

Girdled by wooded hills in the countryside, twenty minutes by bus or taxi from the town of Suwon, the village comprises 240 cottages, villas, administrative offices, taverns and other buildings, as well as a lake, a stream, a bridge, an open-air performance space and abundant tea shops and restaurants. Many of the buildings date back to the Yi dynasty, having been transported from far and near and then reconstructed; even those that are of more recent date at least *look* that old.

But the folk village is more than a museum of old buildings, for in many of them you can see craftspeople, not waxworks this time, at work in the old way. Here's a carpenter, pulling the plane towards him as he smoothes a plank. Under the eaves of that cottage two women are spinning silk from the cocoons bubbling in a cauldron. Elsewhere you'll see blacksmiths forging traditional tools with hammer and anvil, a scholar practicing calligraphy in his study, a young woman wearing *hanbok* pounding rice into flour in an old stone mortar. The criminals in the

jail and the cows in the cow shed are fakes - but the chickens strutting officiously around are for real, as is the priest who takes care of the Buddhist temple. A pounding of drums draws you to the dirt ring near the center of the village where you find a big crowd gathered to watch a vivid folk dance, the boys with paper tapes flying from their caps swirling round and round the space like toy tops.

The folk village is a theme park in a sense, a huge open-air drama which takes place simultaneously on dozens of different stages. But what gives it the edge on Disneyland is that it's almost for real. The craftspeople, one senses, are perfectly at home with their tasks: those women spinning silk have surely been doing it all their lives. And it's not only the performers who seem natural and at home here; the visitors, the great majority Korean, may be wearing Western clothes, but they are a generation or less away from these traditional realities. Young girls attack the bouncing see-saw with hilarious abandon, their elders sit and fan themselves on the ve-

107

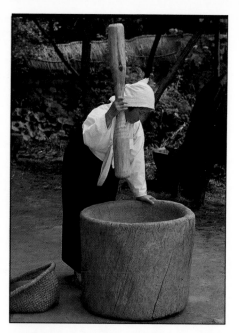

randahs of old cottages, or tackle feasts of *anju* and great bowls of *makkolli* in the taverns at the far end of the site. After a while any sense of distance between visitors and village evaporates.

The Folk Village is thus an ideal introduction to traditional Korea, and whets the appetite for more adventurous forays into the interior - though nowhere does the old way of life survive in quite the pristine way it is presented here.

Before or after seeing the village, it's worth spending some time in **Suwon** itself. Near the end of the eighteenth century King Chongjo resolved to move his capital from Seoul to this city, and in preparation he ordered a great fortress, the "Flower Fortress," built here and the city to be enclosed by massive walls. This was all done according to his will but somehow he never got around to making the move, and during the Korean War the whole lot was destroyed. In 1975, however, the government decided to rebuild it ac-

ABOVE Aristocratically costumed attendants LEFT and rice-pounding farmer RIGHT at Suwon's Korean Folk Village.

cording to the original design. Four and a half years and $3.3 billion dollars later the project was completed. The walls, five and a half kilometers (nearly three and a half miles) in length, and the fortress may be freely inspected.

King Chongjo was a scholar and aesthete as well as a builder, and if you stroll up to the North Gate you can catch one of his happiest effects. Just below a pretty octagonal pavilion is an exquisitely landscaped pond. The king apparently liked to relax in the pavilion with the ladies of the court and enjoy watching the reflection of the moon crossing the pond's surface.

Suwon is easily reached from Seoul. Take the subway from City Hall - make sure you catch the right one, with Suwon in *han'gul* on the front - and it will take you all the way, mostly overground. Tickets to the Folk Village can be bought near Suwon Station. On leaving the station cross the road in front of you by the underpass. On the left hand side and a few doors up is the office of the Folk Village, framed by two totem poles. A ticket to the village costs ₩2,500, which includes the cost of the bus there and back. Buses leave for the village from right outside the office.

P'ANMUNJOM: WINDOW TO THE NORTH

P'anmunjom is the only place where North and South Korea meet. Here, on the site of a farming village destroyed in the civil war, in a blue-painted hut built of breeze blocks with a corrugated iron roof which straddles the military demarcation line (DMZ), representatives of the two sides have been eyeballing and stonewalling each other for more than thirty years. In one meeting it is

recorded that the North Koreans referred to the United States as the "US Imperialist Aggressor" more than 300 times.

A trip to P'anmunjom is hardly a barrel of laughs, but it is one that no visitor to the country should miss. The only way to do it is on an official tour, arranged by the Korea Tourist bureau which has an office in the Lotte Hotel. It is necessary to book forty-eight hours in advance, presenting your passport at the same time, and tours are often canceled for "security reasons", so be prepared to try and try again. Tour members are not allowed to wear jeans, sneakers or other sloppy clothes, presumably to avoid handing the North ready-made propaganda about Western decadence. Setting off at 9 am, buses return to central Seoul by about 4 pm.

The trip builds slowly during the thirty-five mile ride from Seoul to the DMZ. Beyond the northern suburbs ordinary countryside surrounds you. Then in the middle of a field is a stalled loco-

Traditional methods of smithying ABOVE and paper-making LEFT demonstrated at Suwon's Folk Village.

motive, stalled for thirty years, with notrack to take it further north. In the old days it used to be possible to ride a train all the way from Pusan to Paris.

There are the memorials - to Filipinos who died in the war, to Korean soldiers who deliberately blew themselves up, the world's only memorial to dead foreign correspondents. There is the **House of Nostalgia**, where Koreans hold memorial services and pray for re-unification. Some ten million Koreans suffered family break-ups because of the war. The House of Nostalgia is as close to the DMZ as ordinary south Korean citizens are allowed to go.

Five hundred meters (546 yards) south of the DMZ, at Camp Kitty Hawk, base camp for the United Nations Command Support Group which patrols the DMZ, an American soldier takes over from the Korean guide. After a briefing in the camp and a lunch of roast beef and mashed potatoes in the NCO Mess, the bus takes you to the heart of the matter, the **Joint Security Area**, where more than 400 official meetings have been held since 1953 - the longest continuing peace talks in history.

Visitors can wander about inside the Military Armistice Commission buildings which straddle the Military Demarcation Line; it is even possible to cross into North Korea (the far side of the conference table), and you may take snaps of the North Korean guards peering in at you through the windows.

Apart from the military, the only people living in the DMZ are the farmers of the South Korean village of Taesong-dong. The lives they lead are tightly circumscribed: they must be back in the village by dusk each day and at home and accounted for by 11 pm. In compensation they are among the wealthiest farmers in the country, owning far more land than the average, and are exempt from income tax and military service.

North Korea has its DMZ village,

too, and a brief bus ride away from the Joint Security Area visitors get a good view of it. It's a much grander-looking affair than Taesong-dong, with many four-story brick houses, but it's a sham, built solely to counter-balance the real village in the south. Some fifteen to twenty workers commute here every day to raise and lower the vast flag and turn the lights in the houses on and off, but no-one lives here. That's one reason why the US troops call it Propaganda Village. The other is that loudspeakers in the village bombard the south with the praises of Kim Il-sung six to twelve hours a day, mostly at night.

There is really nothing to *see* at P'anmunjom, nothing of beauty or antiquity, but it is certainly a gripping trip. It offers a rare opportunity to see through the veil of comfortable illusions behind which we live our lives, to the tense and weird rivalry which is behind it. Here, where irreconcilable enemies sharing the same blood and often the same names spend their days in such close proximity - nearly standing on each others' toes in the Joint Security Area - that you might mistake them for

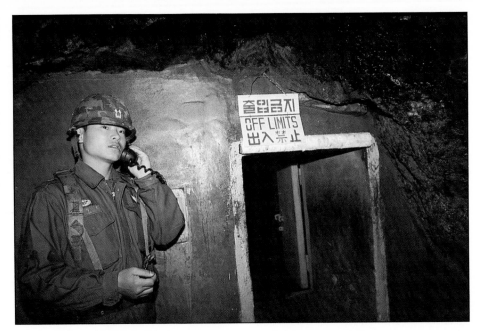

best buddies except that they are armed to the teeth, one gets a vivid sense of the fragility of peace; for if any of these men were to do anything violently unexpected the result could, within days or hours, be the end of life on earth as we know it. This is the reality of the modern world, and it is frequently indistinguishable from the weirdest fantasy. Take the DMZ, for example, which is in fact not demilitarized at all, but one of the most intensively militarized places on earth: despite the million soldiers gathered on either side of it in tense readiness, it has been so uninterruptedly peaceful for more than thirty years that the native bears, wildcats, deer and cranes of Korea have decided that it is the most comfortable place in the country to live. The whole strip has become the peninsula's greatest wildlife sanctuary.

KANGHWA-DO: ISLAND OF EXILE

About 50 km (31 miles) northwest of Seoul, just south of the DMZ and linked to the mainland by bridge, Kanghwa Island has cultural relics spanning Korea's entire history, including prehistoric dolmen, one of the country's oldest temples, and the restored palace of the Yi dynasty king who took refuge there.

Buses leave regularly for Kanghwa-do (*do* means island) from Seoul's Sinchon Rotary, and the trip takes about one-and-a-half hours.

As you cross Yomha Strait to enter the island you'll notice the remains of walls and fortresses constructed during the mid-thirteenth century. These were built to protect the royal family, who took refuge there during the Mongol invasions. **Kanghwa City** lies just beyond these fortifications.

The town itself is small and rustic, a perfect place for leisurely strolls. Here you'll find some of Korea's best floor mats, doorway screens and rush baskets for sale. The town is also an important silk-weaving center.

Next to the silk factory, hanging in a small pavilion, is a 3,864 kg (8,518 lb) bronze bell cast during the reign of King Sukchong (1674-1720). When

ABOVE and LEFT P'anmunjom's "Tunnels of Aggression", driven four kilometers through solid rock by the North.

111

French troops stormed the island in 1866 in a punitive raid to avenge the execution of nine French Catholic priests in Seoul, they tried to carry away this bell as booty, but found it too heavy and abandoned it before reaching their ships.

Further up the road is the restored palace of **King Kojong**, who spent twenty-eight years in retreat here as the Koryo dynasty tried unsuccessfully to resist the Mongol invasions. Lower down the hill, along a narrow pathway, is one of Kanghwa's most interesting structures: Korea's oldest **Episcopal Church**, built in 1900 by Bishop Charles Korfe. The architecture combines Chinese, Christian and Korean motifs, and the symbols which embellish it reflect Taoist, Buddhist and Christian influences.

En route back to town you might care to visit the **dolmen** (sacred altar) constructed of three enormous flat stones and erected during the Bronze Age. Though little is known about the lives or beliefs of its builders, it bears a strong resemblance to megaliths found in western Europe, especially in Brittany.

On the southern part of the island stands Mt Mani, with Tan-gun's Altar a its summit. Though the actual history of the altar is obscure, the story goes that Tan-gun, creator of Korea, built it himself in the course of that seminal act. The 500 m (550 yard) climb to the top is worth it for the panoramic views.

Sixteen kilometers (10 miles) south of the town and two kilometers (one and a quarter miles) east of Mt Mani stands **Chongdung-sa**, one of the oldest temples in the country, built in 381. It was here that the 80,000 woodblocks of the *Tripitaka Koreana*, the canon of sacred Buddhist writings, were carved, a mammoth task which

took sixteen years to finish. There is also a large iron bell of Chinese origin, cast in 1097 during the Northern Sung dynasty. Most interesting of all are the four human figures, squatting uncomfortably with their knees pressed up against their chins, which hold up the eaves of the main hall. It's said that the vengeful builder carved them this way after his beautiful fiancée ran off with a younger man. The images represent the girl, naked and crouching in eternal pain as she holds up the roof of the main hall.

For those with a taste for temples, there is one more excursion worth making on Kanghwa Island. Take the ferry from Uip'o-ri on Kanghwa's west coast to nearby **Songmo Island**. Next comes a jolting forty-five minute bus ride up to **Pomun-sa**, a 1,400-year-old temple which has been beautifully restored. The site commands a fine view of the Yellow Sea and the numerous islands which dot it. In a stone chamber behind the temple sit twenty-two stone Buddha images, each enshrined in a wall-niche. One last, strenuous hike takes you up to the famous "Eyebrow Rock" Buddha, carved into a sheer granite cliff, from

ABOVE Chilies drying outside a farm in western Korea.

where he gazes serenely into the setting sun over the Yellow Sea.

BEYOND SEOUL:

THE HAEIN TEMPLE AND TAEGU

Taegu, the republic's third largest city, is three-and-a-half hours south of Seoul by bus or train and has a population of about one million. The main reason for coming here is to see the ancient **Haein Temple,** one hour by bus out of the city to the west.

Set in the thickly-forested foothills of Mt Gaya, a national park, Haein-sa is one of the greatest centers of Buddhist scholarship in the Orient, and a temple that every visitor to Korea should see. Not only does it have a rich history but it is still a vital monastic center, and the setting of densely forested mountains makes it easy to imagine that one has been transported back 1,000 years, to Korean Buddhism's heyday.

This is how the temple came to be built: in the year 802, two devout monks made a pilgrimage to China, and

on their return they went into retreat in the forests of Mt Gaya. Not long afterwards the wife of King Aejang fell ill, and when the court physicians proved unable to help her, the king turned in desperation to these two monks, who were known throughout the realm for their purity and austerity. The monks effected a miraculous cure, and in a spirit of pious gratitude the king built a great temple for them, close by their mountain hermitage. Haein-sa was the name given it, the Temple of the Reflection of the Sea; the Buddha's wisdom being compared to a sea so calm that it reflects like a mirror. This is an important image in the theology of the Hwaom sect to which Haein-sa belongs.

The temple complex consists of 50 major buildings besides 13 hermitages hidden away in the surrounding hills. From the cluster of new souvenir shops where the bus drops you, a broad winding path leads up the mountainside to the entrance gates of the temple proper. Within, in the central courtyard, stands a fine triple-tiered pagoda and a stone lantern, both erected in 808, soon after the temple's construction. The **Nine Lights Pavilion**, at the front side of this courtyard, contains a small museum of relics from the temple's past, including a life-size, three-dimensional self-portrait of a cadaverously grinning abbot.

The main hall houses a bronze image of the Vairocana Buddha, while on either side are icons representing the wisdom and practice of Buddhism. To the left of the main hall stands the **Hall of Judgment,** with images of the Ten Judges and graphic depictions of the various hells reserved for the various categories of sinner. On either side of the central courtyard are blocks of cells, accommodation for the resident monks, and you may see book stands set on the verandah outside holding volumes of the sutras. There are currently over 250

113

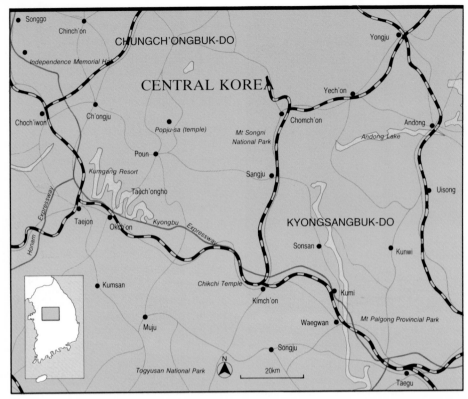

monks and nuns in residence at Haein-sa, about half of them studying the ancient Scriptures stored there, the other half sitting in meditation in the various hermitages. It certainly feels like a very lived-in temple. Peek into the big, earth-floored kitchen and you may see a young monk stoking the fire under the old-fashioned cauldrons with logs. You may also see masons and carpenters at work, for the temple is continuously being restored and renovated using stone and lumber culled from the surrounding mountains.

Up the steep steps behind the main hall is Haein-sa's chief claim to fame: the long, grilled wooden storehouse which contains the tens of thousands of wood blocks on which are inscribed the *Tripitaka Koreana*, the Korean canon of Buddhist scripture.

Commissioned by King Kojong in 1236 while exiled on Kanghwa Island during the Mongol occupation, the pur-

pose of the undertaking was to enlist the aid of Buddhist gods in ridding Korea of the Mongols. The text was based on the original and complete Chinese translation of the Buddhist Tripitaka, which was subsequently lost in China. "Tripitaka" means "Three Baskets," these being "sutra," discourse, the Buddha's words; "viyana," discipline, the rules of Buddhist practice; and "apid-harma," "analysis," philosophical discussions about the sutra by Buddhist scholars.

The white-birch wood blocks, each measuring twenty-nine inches long, nine-and-a-half inches wide and two-and-a-half inches thick, were imported from China and had to be seasoned for nine years before they could be used. After that, twenty scribes and 180 wood carvers labored for ten years to inscribe the complete Tripitaka on 80,000 of these blocks, with no errors or deletions. Buddhist scholars from other countries still visit the temple to study them.

The library which houses them is the oldest building in the temple and dates from 1488. Two devastating fires which destroyed everything else left the library unscathed, a miracle attributed to divine protection. The library is ingeniously constructed: its altitude is 750 m (2,690 ft), exactly mid-way between sea level and the summit of Mt Gaya. Cold air from the mountain-top and warm air from the valley floor meet at this point, providing an ideal atmosphere for the blocks, and the library is thoroughly ventilated by latticed windows, which ensure optimum circulation of air inside. Elevated shelves and deep troughs prottect the collection against flooding. Under the foundations lie thick layers of charcoal, lime and salt, which absorb excess moisture during the humid summers and release it back into the library during the dry winters. The library is, in other words, a masterpiece of air-conditioning technology which requires no moving parts. A few years ago a thoroughly modern library was built nearby, complete with electric fans, automatic vents, dehumidifiers and thermostats – but after a while the monks discovered thatt the blocks they had experimentally stored there had begun to deteriorate. All were returned to the original library, where they can be expected to survive the next 500 years as immaculately as the first.

Besides the main temple complex there are many other places worth visiting in **Mt Gaya National Park,** where the dense forests, rushing streams and sparkling waterfalls make for exhilarating hiking. Five hundred meters (550 yards) beyond the main temple, for example, you'll find the **Hongje-Am Hermitage;** others nearby include **Geumseon-Am** and **Gugil-Am,** both for nuns, and **Bohyeon-Am.** Two kilometers (one and a quarter miles) west of the temple is a tranquil wooded retreat by a cool pool formed by Yongmun waterfall,

while deeper into the hills is a famous seven and a half meter (25 ft) tall image of Buddha carved out of a solid lump of granite, which dates from the eighth century. Those with the stamina might like to hike up to the summit of Mt Gaya and admire the terrific views from the antique Jeonmang-Dae Observatory. **Naghwa Lake,** near the Gilsang-Am Hermitage, is considered to be one of Mt Gaya's "seven scenic sights," while the **Nongsam-Jeong Pavilion,** high up in a grove of pines, stands above a stream bed of spectacular boulders, over

which the mountain waters cascade lustily down to the valleys below.

Winding back down the mountain from Haein-sa — note the umbrella-shaded pit-stops on the way where monks can be observed eating ice creams — you arrive back at the road where the bus dropped you. Ten minutes further on is the little resort village which lives off the tourists visiting the temple. It has over a dozen inns and numerous restaurants and bars, and is the obvious place to spend a night or two if you decide to give Mt Gaya a proper going over. The restaurants here specialize in the wild mushrooms and vegetables which are picked in the mountains, gathered from the surround-

Main hall of Haein-sa Temple: exterior shot.

ing wilderness.

A particularly charming inn here is the **Kook Geh Inn** which overlooks the rest of the village from its vertiginous perch. Built entirely of wood in classical Korean style, it's hard to miss if you walk up through the village.

If you prefer to see Haein-sa and return to the city within one day, it's simply done as the buses are frequent and **Taegu,** much the closest city, has plenty of decent accommodation. Though short on important things to see, Taegu is a prosperous and cheerful place, famous for its apples and its herbal medicine market, one of Korea's biggest.

The apples were introduced during the nineteenth century by an American missionary, James Adams, and are well-known throughout the Far East for their crispness. To see mountains of them visit Taegu's **West Gate Market,** one of the oldest and most colorful bazaars in Korea. Taegu is the major market center for most of Korea's southern provinces, and the market gives a good idea of the incredible volume and variety of produce that pours through the town. The medicine market, **Yak-chong Kolmok,** known to foreigners as Medicine Lane, is an equally eye-opening sight, with its herbs and roots, its dried and stretched reptiles and its bundles of insects.

Taegu's increasing affluence is apparent in the many new buildings which line its broad, leafy streets, its massive new churches and the liveliness of the center at night. The area south of Taegu Station (not Dong-Taegu, **East Taegu,** which is where the trains from Seoul stop) is bursting with evidence of prosperity – shop windows crammed full of cakes, vendors' bowls overflowing with strawberries, chic little interior shops selling stripped pine furniture and fancy lamp stands, cafes and night clubs *à la Japonaise*. Standing with your back to the entrance of the Dong-in Hotel, walk down to the right and take the first right turn and you'll find yourself on **Dong Sung Road,** Taegu's "Broadway," its lanes solid with eating and drinking establishments – *makkolli* bars, beer-halls,

Gorgeous interior of Haein-sa Temple's main hall.

restaurants, cafes, salons and clubs. Among Taegu's more improbable temptations is the ornate new French restaurant "**Avignon**," just down the lane from the rear entrance of the Dong-In Hotel, groaning under the weight of its crystal chandeliers, marble trim and rococo detailing. The food is passable.

The other recommended downtown hotel is **Hanil Hotel**, but there are abundant inns - *yogwan* and *yoinsook* - near Taegu Station which offer simple but decent and cheap accommodation.

Places to visit in the Taegu area, besides Haein-sa, include **Apsan Park**, with its cable car running to the peak of Mt Ap for sweeping views over the Taegu plain; **Si-Sung Reservoir** on the southern edge of the city, popular for boating in summer and skating in winter; the Shilla period **Tonghwa Temple**, a thirty-minute drive north of the city, on the steep slopes of Palgong Mountain which offers excellent hiking possibilities; and the pretty little temple called **Yong-yon**, thirty minutes in the opposite direction, which is also set in an area famous for its hiking trails. A little further afield is **Chikchi Temple**, a seven kilometer (four and one third mile) bus or cab ride from the town of Kimchon, halfway between Taegu and Taejon. The temple buildings date back to 1602, though it was founded much earlier. Its most famous abbot was Samyong-Taesu, the high-priest who led an army of warrior-monks against the Japanese during the invasion of 1592-98.

KYONGJU: VALLEY OF THE SHILLA KINGS

Kyongju is one place in Korea where the ancient past starts into life wherever you go. Still perhaps wrestling with the look and feel of the most recent Yi dynasty, still baffled by the different invasions and divisions, the visitor who stays a day or two here soon finds himself enthralled by and overwhelmingly curious about the much older culture of Shilla, of which Kyongju was the heart.

All told the Shilla era lasted nearly a thousand years, from 57 BC to AD 935, and this town, then called Sorabol, was the kingdom's capital throughout. Relics of that long period are richly scattered through the valley. Eclipsed for over a thousand years when succeeding dynasties made their capitals elsewhere, Kyongju's ancient heritage has only recently been re-discovered.

Modern Kyongju is a typical, rather run-down Korean country town, with enough inns, restaurants and bars to keep the visitor amused when he's not exploring the sights but with little of intrinsic interest - though south of the center there are a lot of traditionally roofed houses. Traditional roofs have become a bit of a fad here since the town was identified as one of the country's most important tourist destinations. Even some of the gas stations have them.

The area's real attractions are nearly all well over a thousand years old, and what is amazing is how many there are. Two or three days is long enough to see the most famous and striking places, but those whose curiosity is fired will find it possible to come back time and time again without exhausting Kyongju's possibilities. For such people, *Korea's Kyongju* by Edward Adams (grandson of the man who introduced apples into Taegu) will be helpful. It's full of extraordinary yarns from the Shilla period. The price is ₩10,000 and it's available at Kyongju's National Museum.

Kyongju's ruins are widely scattered, so unless one is traveling in a chauffeur-driven limousine it's wise to plan routes carefully. The following four itineraries require a minimum of taxi and/or bus rides and only a moderate amount of walking.

First Itinerary: Central Kyongju

Tumuli Park: The assembly of gentle green mounds south-west of Kyongju Station is the burial ground of King Michu (reigned 262- 283) and of at least twenty other Shilla kings. The park was created in 1973 when 180 encroaching dwellings were removed and the whole area enclosed and landscaped. Juniper, pine and bamboo, traditional Korean symbols of longevity, are dotted around the park.

Since its opening in 1973, Tumuli Park has yielded 11,526 priceless relics, which are now on display in the national museums of Kyongju and Seoul. Most of them came from the **Tomb of the Heavenly Horse,** *Cheonma* in Korean, where replicas of some of the precious items found are displayed in wall niches. Visitors are free to enter and inspect although the bones of the king interred here have long since disintegrated, owing to the acidity of the soil. His solid gold crown, his belt of beaten gold, his jade ornaments and other possessions were found intact in their original positions when the tomb was opened.

The crown is without question the

most glorious of these wonderful treasures, and is of a beauty and sophistication that has few parallels in East Asia or indeed anywhere else in the world.

OPPOSITE A section of Pulguk-sa Temple, near Kyongu. TOP Bomun Lake resort, near Kyongju. BOTTOM RIGHT Distinctive massive stone frontage of Pulguk-sa Temple, Kyongju.

More than just an extraordinary work of art, it's a dense mass of symbolism. The three tall structures at the front represent cosmic pine trees, the two at the back represent reindeer antlers, and both of these are important symbols of longevity as well as ancient signs of shaman power. The whole crown is covered with comma-shaped pendants of jade, which represent the claws of the tiger, the most potent repeller of evil influences.

The Tomb of the Heavenly Horse is the only one of the 20 burial chambers to have been excavated so far, and

under the Shilla banner. The park was originally conceived as a sort of scale model of the united Shilla Kingdom, complete with rivers and mountains, seas and lagoons, pavilions and palaces. It was here in 935 that the last Shilla king finally surrendered to invading forces, bringing the dynasty to an end eight years short of a millennium from its inception. Repaired and restored in 1975, Anapchi Pond is a pleasant park which retains some echoes of its days of glory – though inevitably restoration fell far short of recreating the garden as it used

visitors may feel that the show is a little thin considering the price of admission. Most of Kyongju's other sights are certainly better value – but no other place puts one so thoroughly into the Shilla frame of mind.

A few hundred yards from Tumuli Park to the east is **Anapchi Pond,** the site of royal pleasure pavilions where Shilla kings fished for carp and went boating with concubines, composing verse the while. It was constructed in 674 under the auspices of King Munmu, to celebrate the unification of Korea

to be.

Ten minutes from here on foot is the institution that helps one to make sense of everything else in Kyongju, the **National Museum.** A bold attempt to unite Shilla and modern taste in one design, the museum has a fabulous collection of artifacts from all over the area, including bronze, ceramic, decorated roof-tiles and more of the incredible gold jewelry mentioned above.

In a separate pavilion outside the museum hangs the famous **Emille Bell** (pronounced *emil-leh*), one of the largest and (they say) most resonant bells in Asia. It was cast over 1,000 years ago, and a sad story attaches to its creation. It seems that the bell-maker tried over and over again to cast it to the king's specifications, but each time the newly-finished bell was struck it cracked. He was at his wits' end and on the verge of committing suicide when an old monk appeared and told his widowed sister that her brother's task could be accomplished and his life saved only through the sacrifice of her infant daughter. The virtuous sister resolved

to do her bitter duty, and despite the compassionate bell-maker's entreaties insisted that he do as the monk said. Finally he consented: he carried the hapless baby to his workshop and flung her into the molten metal! When the bell was finally cast, not only did it not crack but its tone was painfully beautiful, reminiscent of a baby's plangent wailing. Hence the bell's name, Emille, which is the old Shilla language's onomatopoeic word for a baby's cry.

This fascinating story combines the ever-popular Confucian theme of the conflict of duty and human feelings with a human sacrifice motif which harks back to Shilla's much older shamanist tradition. The Shilla kingdom was the last part of the peninsula to accept Buddhism, and shamanist influence was slow to fade.

Visitors unfortunately have little op-portunity to corroborate this story, as the bell is rarely if ever rung.

Those with the stamina may finish off this first excursion, after a walk of about 25 minutes, with a visit to **Bunhwang-sa Pagoda.** This small temple boasts the oldest surviving pagoda in Korea. Built in 634 under the auspices of Shilla's Queen Sondok, the pagoda displays superb relief carvings and guardian statues. Originally nine stories high, the three remaining levels are built entirely of stones cut to the size of, and resembling, bricks. In the courtyard is a Fountain of Youth, and whether or not the water adds years to your life, it certainly tastes pure. A 1,300-year-old gilt Buddha graces the main prayer-hall, and the grouunds are beautifully landscaped with flowering fruit trees, pine, juniper, bamboo and weeping willow.

Second Excursion: South-east

Pulguk-sa and Sokkuram: 16 km (10 miles) south-east of Kyongju, built on distinctive platforms high on a steep hillside at the end of a long and winding approach road, Pulguk-sa is arguably Korea's most impressive and popular temple complex.

Established in 528 by a minister of the Shilla court, the temple was expanded to its present proportions in 751. There have been 23 reconstructions since then, the latest completed in 1973. The present temple is about one-tenth the size of the original complex.

Pulguk-sa is set in a glade of pine and juniper trees. The various halls, pavilions and shrines are located in walled compounds which climb up the hillside, and from the top the temple roofs form a sea of tile. In the main

OPPOSITE Traditional roofs are found everywhere in Kyongju - by government decree. ABOVE Entrance to Flying Horse Tomb in Kyongju's Tumuli Park.

courtyard stand two large pagodas which are considered to be the best surviving examples of Shilla masonry in Korea. The more ornate **Tabotop Pagoda** represents the ascent of man from a base condition to the purity and perfection of Buddhist enlightenment. Opposite stands the strong, masculine **Sokkat'ap Pagoda**, which symbolizes man's descent into the earthly realm. Both are over a thousand years old.

In the main prayer hall sits a large gilt Buddha, and up the steps behind the main hall, in the top corner of the complex, is a delightful small shrine hall dedicated to Kuan Yi, Goddess of Mercy. This hall is a particularly graceful and compact example of traditional Korean temple architecture at its very best.

The Sokkuram Buddha: Up the road from Pulguk-sa, high on a mountain peak which commands panoramic views of the East Sea and the Kyongju Valley, is **Sokkuram**, the "Cave of the Stone Buddha." To get there used to re-

quire a long, hard climb up mountain paths, but today a smooth road winds all the way to the top. Mini-buses from Pulguk-sa leave frequently, and the return fare is included in the cost of admission to Sokkuram. For those to whom the word "pilgrimage" still means something, however, the walk is to be recommended. It puts you in a properly receptive frame of mind for the marvel that awaits you at the top.

From the summit parking lot, a wooded path twists for several hundred meters along the side of the mountain, then takes a final dip and you have arrived. From the lower courtyard with its Fountain of Youth (yes, another one), whose waters are believed to be capable of prolonging one's life by ten years, steep steps climb to the object of the journey, the **Sokkuram grotto**.

The exterior is extraordinary enough; either this building has just been three-quarters buried in a rock-slide, one would guess, or else it is mysteriously emerging from the heart of the mountain. Inside, seated on a lotus dias, is what many who ought to know regard as the most aesthetically perfect, sub-

ABOVE Kyongju coffee shop. Tile roofs and vinyl sleeves against the mesmerizing green of Kyongju's plain. OPPOSITE Honeymoon couple posing at Kyongju's Pulguk-sa Temple.

122

limely tranquil image of Sakyamuni Buddha ever executed. A marvel of form and proportion, the white granite Buddha faces east toward the East Sea and the rising sun. Even children are awed and silenced by the sight.

The cave-grotto is an elaborate frozen drama on a theme of Buddhist mythology. The entrance hall is guarded by eight fearsome generals in stone relief and two wild-looking guardians in classical martial arts poses. Four Deva Kings protect the inner portal. In a circle around the Buddha are relief images of the Ten Great Disciples and the Eight Great Bodhisattvas.

Due to the large number of visitors, the images are protected behind glass; but the lighting is subtle and nice, and it's arguable that the glass screen only enhances the powerful impression made by the Buddha.

Frequent buses run from Kyongju (passing close to the station) to Pulguk-sa; two of them are numbers 15 and 35. On the left as you approach Pulguk-sa after leaving the main road is Kyongju's **Youth Hostel**, one of the most popular cheap places to stay in the

area (it's gigantic), and a little further on is the **Kolon Hotel**, which has a casino. Some of Kyongju's most attractive accommodation, however, is provided in the artificial village at the foot of Pulguk-sa's mountain. The tourist center has numerous shops, cafes and restaurants as well as over a dozen *yogwan*, all designed Shilla style. The price of accommodation is more reasonable than in Lake Pomun's hotels (see below), and the location is ideal for those who would like to take their time exploring the immediate area. Cheaper accommodation, if the price is crucial, is to be found among the *yogwan* and *yoinsook* in the back-streets of Kyongju itself.

A side-trip from Pulguk-sa takes you back down to the main road and then left (south-east) for another four kilometers (two and a half miles) to **Kwaenung Tomb**. Far less frequented than Pulguk-sa, the tomb's mound is entirely encircled by beautifully carved stone reliefs depicting the twelve animals of the Oriental zodiac. What makes this site even more worthwhile are the rows of stone statues which guard the approach to the tomb. Soldiers, civil officials and lions stand in perpetual protective vigil before the tomb of their royal master. The wavy hair, heavy beards and prominent noses of the military figures were probably inspired by the Persian mercenaries who are known to have served at the Shilla court.

Third Excursion: South
Onung Tombs: To the south of the town lie five of Shilla's most ancient tombs, including the tomb of the king who founded the dynasty. There are also several shrines erected here in honor of the founding king, who is said to have been born here from a golden egg left by a horse which flew down from heaven with it. Hidden in a clump of pine and bamboo is another shrine dedicated to Shilla's first queen, who was born, the story goes, from the rib of a dragon.

A fair hike down the main road brings you to **Posokdong Bower**, once the site of an elaborate Shilla pleasure palace. All that remains today is a granite trough shaped somewhat like an abalone (*posok* in Korean). Set in a shady glade, this trough used to be the focus of drunken royal revelries. The king with his entourage of courtiers and concubines would sit around the stone trough while dancers performed for them. Without warning the king would deliver a spontaneous line of poetry, and command one of the courtiers to come up with an appropriate line to match it. At the same time he would set a large bowl of wine afloat in the trough, and if the courtier had not managed to think of something suitable by the time the bowl reached him, he was obliged to drink it down in one. And so it continued, with predictable results - though one one day in 927 the game went seriously awry when it was interrupted by a band of rebels, who retreated only after slaying the king and sacking his palace.

Another good walk away, due south

this time, in a grove of pine trees on a hillside, stand the three mysterious images known as the **Triple Buddhas**. First discovered lying askew on the slopes of nearby Namsan in 1923, these statues display none of the stylistic characteristics of classical Shilla statuary, but rather reflect the massive proportions and bold lines of the northern Koguryo style. No-one knows how they got to the Kyongju Valley. Today they are kept in a walled grotto and looked after by a family who maintain a small shrine in their honor.

Fourth Excursion: Lake Bomun
The attractions of Kyongju are almost exclusively ancient ruins - but not quite. There is one exception. If you are traveling with children and they are gradually becoming cheesed off - or if you yourself could do with a change of mood - head for the new Lake Bomun resort center, a few kilometers due east of the city.

The center is an ambitious project: if the Korean government's plan is realized, Kyongju will before long become a major international resort, as well as a "museum without walls." Currently there are four deluxe hotels by the shores of the artificial lake, with ten more planned, and a children's amusement park on the far side. The lakeside grounds are pleasantly landscaped, and there are big swan boats to take visitors for rides across the lake.

The four day-trips outlined above will give the visitor a good feeling for what Kyongju is all about. Other sites which will repay the small trouble involved in getting there include the following:

Tomb of General Kim Yu-shin
North west of the city center is the tomb of one of Korea's outstanding military heroes. Along with King Muyol, whose armies he led during Shilla's

seventh century campaigns to unify Korea's "Three Kingdoms," he is regarded as one of the "Three Unifiers," the veritable founding fathers, of the Korean nation. General Kim also led Korea's united forces in repulsing a bid by the armies of T'ang China to conquer the emerging Korean nation.

Though smaller than King Muyol's tomb (see below), the tomb of General Kim displays a far greater sophistication of design. Encircled by superbly carved figures from the Oriental zodiac, the tomb lies on a wooded bluff overlooking the Kyongju Valley.

Tomb of King Muyol: Southwest of the general's tomb (too far to walk) is a spectacular group of tombs collectively referred to as King Muyol's Tomb. This king, famous for having conquered the Paekche Kingdom and thus paved the way for the unification of the country, is honored by an impressive monument just inside the gate: on a large stone tortoise sits a heavy capstone writhing with intricately carved dragons, the symbol of his royal power. If you follow the path beyond the wooded area around the tomb, you will find splendid views of four more burial mounds standing against a background of open sky and rolling hills. This site also commands a distant view of the city.

Travelers with sufficient time and enthusiasm may like to venture even further off the beaten track to visit **Pagoda Valley, Buddha Valley, T'ap Valley, Kuksa Valley**, or the more remote **Sungbang Valley**, all of which are well within driving distance of Kyongju proper. Not a year goes by without important new discoveries being unearthed in Kyongju, and every holiday in Korea should include a few days here.

Discovering Kyongju is pleasant all the year round, but the best time to go is in autumn. The annual Shilla Cultural Festival is held from 8-10 October, and then the whole valley echoes with the sound of Buddhist rites, farmers' bands, and noisy parades, and the city famous for artists and warriors who are a thousand and more years underground, comes suddenly and vigorously to life.

How To Get There

To get to Kyongju from Seoul you have three choices of transport: you can take the fifty-five minute flight to Taegu, then transfer to a bus for the hour-long ride to Kyongju; take the *saemaul* super-express train from Seoul Station for a pleasant four-and-a-half hour ride through the countryside (only two expresses a day, though); or grab an express bus from Seoul's Kangnam Expressway Bus Terminal, where buses leave for Kyongju every hour between 7 am and 6 pm, covering the distance along the Seoul-Pusan expressway in four-and-a-half hours. If money is no object you might rent a car and drive there, which would solve the problem of how to see all the city's far-flung relics in a limited amount of time.

From Pusan, Kyongju-bound express buses leave every half hour between 7 am and 7:30 pm from the city's Express Bus Terminal, and the ride takes 1 hour 40 minutes. A shuttle bus also runs regularly between Pusan's Kimhae Airport and the Lake Bomun resort. The most interesting way to travel between Kyongju and Pusan in either direction is by chugging steam locomotive, a recently revived service which departs from Pusan daily at 9:30 am and returns daily from Kyongju at 1:10 pm. The three-hour ride costs about ₩2,000. While the engine is a genuine antique steam locomotive complete with billowing black smoke and screeching whistle, the cars have been comfortably refurbished.

If you prefer to see Kyongju with a tour rather than on your own, but have failed to arrange it beforehand, no cause to worry: there is a wide range of day-tours available in Kyongju for "FIT"s (foreign individual travelers). The simplest is a one-and-a-half hour tour of Pulguk-sa and Sokkuram Grotto; the most complicated is a full-day tour of fifteen major sites. For details, contact the information desk of any deluxe hotel, or Kyongju's tourist information center, located right outside the train station (tel: 2-3937).

PUSAN: SECOND CITY

The republic's second largest city and principal seaport, Pusan is a place many visitors will have cause to pass through on business or en route to somewhere else, but its intrinsic attractions are rather scanty. Located on the southeast corner of the peninsula, and enjoying Korea's mildest weather, Pusan was the only city which the Communist forces failed to reach on their initial thrust southward in the civil war. Some four million refugees poured into the city, however, settling on the slopes of its many hills, and thirty years later Pusan still retains something of the roughness

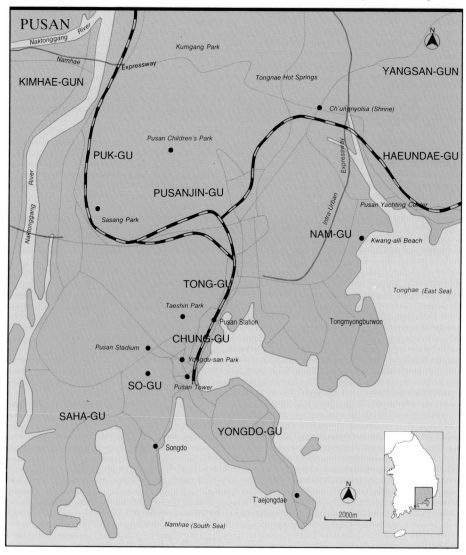

PUSAN

Naktonggang River

Namhae

Kumgang Park

Expressway

Tongnae Hot Springs

KIMHAE-GUN

YANGSAN-GUN

Ch'ungnyolsa (Shrine)

Pusan Children's Park

PUK-GU

HAEUNDAE-GUN

Naktonggang River

Intra-Urban Expressway

PUSANJIN-GU

Pusan Yachting Center

Sasang Park

NAM-GU

Kwang-alli Beach

TONG-GU

Tonghae (East Sea)

Taeshin Park

Pusan Station

Tongmyongburwon

CHUNG-GU

Pusan Stadium

Yongdu-san Park

SO-GU

Pusan Tower

SAHA-GU

YONGDO-GU

Songdo

N

T'aejongdae

2000m

N

Namhae (South Sea)

and desperation of a refugee camp. Or perhaps it's the roughness and desperation of a major port. Or a bit of both. Whichever the case, Pusan is the only city in the country where the visitor should be on the lookout for thieves, pimps and other miscellaneous ne'er-do-wells. Many are the innocent Japanese tourists who have arrived in Pusan by ferry from the Japanese port of Shimonoseki and found themselves taken for long and expensive rides by apparently friendly natives anxious to "practice their Japanese." English speakers may be no less at risk.

Pusan's mountainous setting is dramatic, but with its population of more than three million densely packed for mile after mile, it will continue to be a difficult city to get around in until the subway to the center, presently under construction, is completed.

Central Pusan, where the hotels, banks, central post office and train station are concentrated, is the long, narrow strip that fronts the central harbor, with bus terminals at the northern extreme, the train station near the middle and restaurants, bars and night clubs clustered at the south end. If you arrive on the city's outskirts, the first thing to do is hail a cab and head for this part of town.

It's here, too, that the city sights are to be found. **Pusan Tower,** a tall TV transmission tower in the middle of a pleasant park called **Yongdu-san** (Dragon Head Mountain), at the southern end of the central strip, has an observation deck which commands fabulous views of the city and harbor. A little farther north is the one structure in the city which deserves greater fame: the **Commodore Hotel,** 16 stories of outrageous Yi dynasty kitsch, with up-curving tiled roofs, red lacquered columns, fake wooden bracketing, a massive chandelier made out of lanterns in the lobby and, outside the entrance, a whopping temple bell and hammer (ring for service?). The second floor coffee shop does a passable though expensive pizza,

recommended for homesick connoisseurs of incongruity.

The **fish market** by the harbor is quite a spectacle, and people who take delight in all the comings and goings of a great harbor, the churning of engines and blasting of sirens and smells of seaweed and diesel fumes, will find their time in Pusan flies by. In the evenings the monied may head for the restaurant zone behind Pusan Tower to eat and drink, while those on a budget or intent on sampling the low life will prefer **Texas Street,** the section of bars, discos and hostess clubs, Pusan's

answer to Seoul's It'aewon, which is one street back from the main road and close to **Pusan Station.**

Hot Springs and Beach Resorts

As well as being Korea's major seaport, Pusan is also one of the south coast's most popular beach resorts. While visitors who want to enjoy the best that Korea has to offer would be wise to do their swimming in, say, the resorts of Cheju Island (see P131-140), if you have to be in Pusan for some time, a trip to one of the nearby resorts is certainly an option to consider.

Closest to hand, not far from City Hall and Yongdu-san Park, is **Songdo Beach,** an inexpensive but often crowded local resort. There are no international hotels here, but plenty of inns and restaurants. The beach itself is pleasant and clean, but the water lies a bit too close to the murk of the harbor for comfort.

Pusan: the harbor ABOVE and OVERLEAF the city, sprawling up the flanks of a nearby mountain. At the center is Pusan Tower.

Haeundae, Pusan's most agreeable and up-market beach resort, is eleven miles northeast of the city. Haeundae has several modern hotels, including the deluxe **Chosun Beach Hotel,** said to be one of the best in Korea. A bustling little resort town provides all the facilities of an international resort, and the water is fine. There are hot springs and therapeutic bath-houses in the vicinity as well.

Nine miles north of downtown Pusan is the region's oldest mineral spa, the **Tongnae Hot Springs,** known for its medicinal waters since the late seventeenth century. There are two tourist hotels and several inns nearby. All have mineral baths fed by natural hot springs.

A little to the north of Tongnae is **Kumgang Park,** a region of dense forests, beautiful mountains and curious rock formations. Numerous historical relics are to be found here, including a fortress tower, a pagoda and several temples. A cable-car carries visitors up to the fortress ruins. There is also an amusement park with various carnival rides for children. Kumgang is known as a good place to admire the cherry blossoms in spring.

Side Trips

Two very worthwhile temples are located within easy striking distance of Pusan. **Pomo Temple,** headquarters of the Dyana sect and founded in 678, is a few kilometers north of Tongnae Hot Springs (see above), on the eastern slopes of Mt Kumjong. The temple grounds are beautifully landscaped and dotted with Shilla-era pagodas and stone lanterns.

A little further afield is the **Tongdo Temple,** which is rarely seen by foreign visitors even though it is the nation's largest and one of its most impressive

The seafront TOP and nearby seafood restaurants BELOW at Haeundae Beach in Pusan. OPPOSITE Early morning at Pusan's Songdo beach.

temples. It is located halfway between Pusan and Kyongju along the Seoul-Pusan expressway, and has its own clearly marked exit. The final approach skirts the banks of mountain streams by groves of twisted pine and gnarled juniper. Tongdo-sa has a total of 65 structures, and almost every deity in the Buddhist pantheon has its shrine here. The temple was founded in 646 by a monk-scholar on his return from studying the Scripture of China.

Pusan is also an important launching point for side-trips to other destinations by boat. Ferries run regularly from a terminal located behind City Hall. There are two entrances: the one marked "tourist" provides a fast hydrofoil service with reserved seats; the one marked "common" has a slower service, and it's every man for himself when it comes to securing a seat.

The most popular destination by boat from Pusan is the beautiful Hallyo Waterway, two to three hours southwest of Pusan. Hydrofoils leave for Ch'ungmu six times and Yosu three times a day, with stops at Song'po, Samch'onp'o and Namhae. The trip from Pusan all the way to Yosu takes three-and-a-half hours one way. The slow boat sails once a day with stops at the same places, and takes a little over four hours.

Those wishing to drive in Cheju Island may take their cars over on the car ferry which sails from Pusan every day except Saturdays. And if your next destination after Korea is Japan, the Pukwan Ferry provides a service from Pusan to Shimonoseki. This is much the cheapest way of traveling between the two countries. Like the Cheju service, this ferry also sails every day but Saturday.

If you plan to tour the south coast, especially the Hallyo Waterway, the hydrofoil from Pusan is the pleasantest way to get there. The ride takes you through some of the most beautiful coastal waterways in Asia, with hundreds of green islands formed by the peaks of submerged mountains, and timeless scenes of Korean coastal life. The most popular destination in the Hallyo Waterway is Ch'ungmu, a charming town with a very pleasant tourist hotel, from where you can make further side-trips into the waterway.

Both Cheju Island and the Hallyo Waterway are covered in separate sections, below.

CHEJU-DO: KOREA'S MAGIC ISLAND

In China and Korea there have always been legends telling of an island in the eastern sea where the herb of immortality grows and the people live forever in peace and comfort. Some historians have singled out Taiwan as the magic place, but it could just as well be Cheju Island.

Warm and sunny for much of the year, almost untainted by industry, the roads bordered by carefully-tended flowers, full of curious places to go and things to look at and with a relaxed and outgoing population, Cheju is the outstanding place in Korea for a holiday. More and more people are learning about it, but Cheju has by no means been swamped or spoiled, and the people are as honest and dignified as in the rest of the country.

Located 90 km (56 miles) off the southern coast of the peninsula, and shaped roughly like an egg, Cheju is Korea's largest island, and the republic's only island-province. It is 71 km (44 miles) long and 41 km (25 miles) wide and has a permanent population of about half a million. Volcanic in composition, the island is dominated by the 1,950 m (6,400 ft) lava cone of Mt Halla, the highest peak in South Korea.

Cheju is distinctively different from the mainland. The island's shamanist past is still very evident, with stone altars for performing *kut* (shaman ceremonies) maintained in most villages, and phallic fertility symbols, in the

form of the pop-eyed grandfather images called *Harubang*, made of soapstone, scattered everywhere. Shaman mediums regularly perform seances to exorcise evil spirits, invoke the aid of the gods of fertility or contact the souls of the departed. Cheju is exotic, if that word still possesses any meaning.

The popularity of shamanism in Cheju is related to another distinctive feature of the island: its traditionally matriarchal society. In Cheju it has long been the custom for the men to stay at home and take care of the house while the women go out to work. This in turn is connected with the fact that one of the main sources of wealth and subsistence on Cheju is the sea-bed, and as in Japan and elsewhere it is the women who, for sound physical reasons, have always culled it. The *haenya*, the women divers, are one of the island's enduring attractions, and there are said to be still some 20,000 in business, far more than anywhere else in East Asia (though most of them are part-timers). Ranging in age from ten to sixty, these tough women plunge to depths of 15 to 20 m (45 to 60 ft) and stay under for

ABOVE LEFT Young visitors to Pusan's Tongmyong Burwon Temple. ABOVE RIGHT Food stalls at Pusan's Kukche market.

three to five minutes without the aid of breathing equipment.

Cheju's economy is different from the mainland's in other ways, too. With its relatively mild, almost subtropical climate, the island has become Korea's citrus center, producing oranges, tangerines, grapefruit and pineapples for both domestic and export markets, as well as the "Cheju orange," a hybrid of local and imported species. Cheju's most conspicuous crop is rape (mustard seed), and in spring acre on acre of farmland is vivid with its bright yellow blossom.

Cheju is also Korea's most important region for raising livestock. Much of the country's beef comes from the island, and of the country's 25,000 horses, 17,000 are reared here. At the Isidore Ranch, sheep imported from Japan and New Zealand in the mid-1960s produce enough wool to sustain a thriving cottage industry known as Hallim Handweavers, as well as lamb and mutton for the meat markets.

Until about the year 1000 the island remained aloof from and uninfluenced by events in mainland Korea. During the Koryo dynasty it was given the Korean name "Cheju," which simply means "the district over there." Prior to that its local name had been "Tamna." For centuries the Korean court used Cheju as an island of exile, banishing disgraced officials and criminals to its remote shores, much as the Chinese court used Hainan Island and the Japanese, Sado. Due to this fact, most Koreans regarded the island with a mixture of fear and disdain, if indeed they had heard of it at all.

During the thirteenth century, Cheju was overrun by the Mongols, who brought horses and cattle, raising the former for warfare and the latter for food, and leaving both behind when they were expelled from Korea. The animals thrived in the island's lush pastureland and soon became Cheju's ma-

jor industry.

Cheju was the first place in Korea visited by Westerners, albeit accidentally. On 16 August 1653 the Dutch ship *Sparrow Hawk,* en route from the Dutch enclave in Taiwan to Nagasaki in Japan, ran into a severe typhoon in the straits of Korea and was shipwrecked on the shores of Cheju. The survivors were held there for thirteen years. After their escape to Japan and eventual return to Europe, one of them, Henrik Hammel, wrote a lengthy account of their captivity which was pub-

lished as *The Dutch Come to Korea.* It was the first account of the Hermit Kingdom to appear in the West.

Cheju's role in Korean affairs continued to be peripheral until the mid-1960s, when President Park visited the island and took a personal interest in its development. Since then, Cheju's tourist and industrial infrastructure, and its economic importance to the nation in general, have grown rapidly.

Not only is Cheju one of Korea's biggest tourist resorts, it is also the favorite honeymoon destination for Korean newlyweds. Between thirty-five and forty per cent of all visitors to the island are honeymooners and everywhere you go you'll see them, dressed to the nines and usually accompanied by the taxi driver who doubles as official photographer. Sportsmen come to Cheju to hunt pheasant, deer and wild boar in the mountain game reserves, or

133

to go deep-sea fishing off shore. Others come to loll and swim on the island's dozen beaches, or to hike and camp in the mountains.

CHEJU CITY AND THE NORTHERN SHORE

The island's capital is **Cheju City**, located midway along the northern shore, a town of modest size where the island's mythical founding gods, Ko, Pu and Liang, are believed to have popped out of three holes in the rock. The city has everything the visitor might require in the way of deluxe hotels, restaurants, shops and so on, but most people will probably choose to keep their stay here short. The whole point of Cheju is not its cities but its nature, its mountains, beaches, rocks and flowers, and an overnight stay in the city will normally give enough time to sample the sights and decide where to go next.

For those staying in the city on a budget, the road between the ferry terminal and the market, called **Sanji Ro**, is the place to head for. Many of the city's numerous *yogwan* and *yoinsook* are to be found in the lanes behind this road, and there are also plenty of cheap restaurants here. The bus station is a good hike inland, and the simplest way to get there is by taxi.

Of the things to do in the city, the recently-opened **Cheju Folkcraft and Natural History Museum** can be highly recommended. It gives a useful and attractively designed picture of life in the island, both human and otherwise. The spot where the gods emerged is close by, called **Samsonghyol** ("Cave of the Three Spirits"), and is marked by a shrine.

On the north-western outskirts of town is one of the island's most popular sights, **Yong Du** ("Dragon Head") Rock, an outcrop of basalt formed when molten lava from Mt Halla flowed into the sea and hardened. The

local explanation recalls the popular idea that Cheju was the abode of the immortals: according to this, the Dragon King sent a messenger to Mt Halla, the island's tallest mountain, to obtain the secret Elixir of Immortality from the mountain god. Angered by the intrusion, the latter shot the messenger with an arrow, petrifying him in place by the sea shore.

There are four good swimming beaches along the northern shore. **Samyong Beach**, a ten-minute drive east of the town, and **Hamdok Beach**,

fifteen minutes further east are the most popular and have adequate inns and restaurants. **Kimnyong, Sehwari** and **Kwakji** are smaller, less crowded beaches.

On the north-east corner of the island is one of Cheju's geological wonders, the **Manjang Snake Cave** which, at nearly seven kilometers (four and a third miles), is the longest known lava tube in the world. Three meters at its narrowest and twenty at its broadest, the interior is lit with floodlights and may be explored for about one kilometer (two thirds of a mile) of its length. It's chilly and wet so take a sweater and waterproof shoes. Prior to the seventeenth century, a young female virgin was sacrificed at the entrance of the cave every year to appease the Snake

OPPOSITE Special day for a small resident of Cheju-do. ABOVE High school boys on Cheju in military cadet outfits.

God. This shaman practice was ended in 1625, when a new magistrate arrived from the Korean court. Appalled by the ritual slaughter, he persuaded the locals that he had exorcised the serpent, and then introduced the more civilized Buddhist practice of honoring the spirits with food and wine.

Following the coastal road east we come to **Il-Chul-Bong**, "Sunrise Peak," which is located at Songsanpo, a small village right on the island's eastern tip. A sheer cliff of lava pocked with caves, Sunrise Peak's crater is now a pasture where cows and horses graze, but the views from the tooth-like rocks that stick up around the crater's edge are among the most spectacular on the island. Eastward lies the island of Udo and the shimmering waters of the Straits of Korea. Turn the other way

and you'll see the steep green humps of Cheju's many volcanic peaks poking mistily out of the land's placid roll like islands. To enjoy the area to the full you may feel like staying a night or two here, either at the nearby **Sunrise Hotel** or at one of the simple inns in the village.

Continuing along the coast road then heading inland at Pyosun, we come to a very old Cheju village called **Chongup**. Founded in the fifteenth century, it was formerly the island's capital. Recently it has turned its antiquity to advantage by throwing open several of its humble thatch and soapstone cottages to the public, and now there seems to be a constant coming and going of chauffeured honeymooners. This activity and the restaurants which live off it are confined to one small part of the village, buses ply these routes.

Whichever way you go, traveling to Sogwip'o is a good move, for this is surely one of Korea's prettiest little towns, spread out across a shallow slope which leads to the sea. Sogwip'o is the ideal size for a holiday resort: big enough to have a good range of accommodation, from expensive hotels to simple *yoin-sook*, as well as a lively and fascinating market, yet small enough to be walkable from end to end in fifteen minutes.

A short walk downhill and east of the town center is **Chong-bang Water-**

however, and a short walk away from the action brings one to quiet, dusty little lanes unchanged for centuries, and the recently reconstructed Confucian school.

Chongup is also famous for the two magnificent 1,000-year-old zelkova trees which spread their ample branches near the center of the village.

SOGWIP'O AND THE SOUTHERN SHORE

On the southern shore of the island, directly opposite Cheju City, lies the little town of **Sogwip'o**, famous for its beaches, waterfalls and oranges. You can get there quickly from Cheju City by taking either of the two cross-island highways which skirt the base of Mt Halla, or more slowly by taking the scenic round-the-island road. Frequent

fall, said to be the only waterfall in Asia which drops directly into the sea. A short way to the west, at the end of a charmingly landscaped riverside promenade, is an even more splendid waterfall, **Ch'onjiyon,** though sometimes obscured by the dozens of honeymooners posing in front of it.

Sogwipo is the island's, and hence the nation's, citrus capital, producing oranges, grapefruits and tangerines in great abundance. Protective walls of lava have been built up around the orchards to protect them from the island's constant winds. In addition to citrus, the town has superb sea food, which is served at little restaurants behind the harbor.

A kilometer or so west of Sogwip'o

ABOVE AND LEFT The cloud-covered peaks of Cheju-do's Mt Halla (1,950 m) attract multitudes of hikers.

is **Chungmun Beach**, one of the island's best, just inland of which is the **Hyatt Regency Hotel**, possibly the only place in Cheju where you can have warm croissants for breakfast. Nearby is yet another waterfall, **Chunje-yon**, with a clear, cool pool at the bottom where fairies are said to play. Here also is a memorial in honor of the shipwrecked Dutchmen who were the first Westerners to reach the island. West of Chungmun Beach is another fine bathing area, **Hwasom Beach**, and west of that is **Sambanggul Temple**, an ancient cave hermitage with a handsome seated Buddha.

The Hyatt is a just a foretaste of Chungmun's future, for an extensive resort complex is planned for this area. It will ultimately include ten tourist hotels, six Korean inns, three motels, 130 private villas and three shopping centers, as well as restaurants, bars, cafes, a marina for boating and fishing and other recreational facilities. As a result, Chungmun is bound to lose what little local flavor it now retains, but as long as little Sogwip'o a couple of miles down the road remains largely unchanged, visitors will have no good reason to give up on Cheju.

THE WEST COAST

Coming round the great humped bulk

138

of Mt Sanbang, like the back end of a bison, we swing into Cheju's west coast, where the sea is a lovely turquoise color and, inland, farming couples can be glimpsed shoulder-deep in ripe rice. **Hyopjae Beach** on this side is good for bathing, and close by is **Hyopjaegul Cave,** another well-known lava-tube cavern. But the main attraction on the west coast, one of Cheju's greatest curiosities, is the **Hallim Handweavers' Complex,** in the coastal village of Hallim.

Established more than 20 years ago by Father Patrick McGlinchey, a missionary who has resided in Korea for considerably longer than that, the Hallim Handweavers produce some of the best Irish-style woolens outside of Ireland. The equipment as well as the sheep were brought to the island by Father McGlinchey in the early 1960s, since when the local people have been turning out hand-made sweaters, scarves, caps, mittens and blankets, all in traditional Irish patterns. These rank among Korea's more unlikely souvenirs, and may be bought in Hallim itself or at their special shop in the Chosun Hotel's arcade in Seoul.

Halfway between Hallim and Cheju City you'll find **Hanpaduri,** the remains of a fortress dedicated to the memory of Korea's patriotic *Sambyolch* troops, who refused to capitulate to Mongol suzerainty when the Koryo dynasty surrendered, holding out in this bastion for years before they were finally overwhelmed.

Trekking on Mt Halla

Mt Halla itself is one of the best things on the island, and walking to the top of it one of the "must-dos" for any visitor with a modicum of energy. From where the trail begins on the west side, the walk takes about two-and-a-half hours to the top if you don't stop (which you'll want to) and a little less to get down; from the east side allow about twice as much time. No special equipment is required, only strong shoes or boots and some-

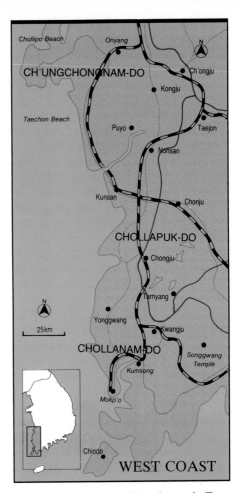

WEST COAST

thing warm, as it is cold at the peak. Free trail maps are available at the ticket offices at the beginning of the trails. (Like most of Cheju's natural attractions, Mt Halla has an admission fee.) Be careful to follow the trails sedulously, as it is quite easy to get badly lost on this mountain if you don't.

Hotels and Transportation

Cheju has hotels and inns to fit every pocket and taste, and more are opening every year. While accommodation can be tight during July and August, in the rest of the year there is no shortage of places to stay.

OPPOSITE ABOVE Sunrise at Il Chul Bong, Sunrise Peak, Songsanpo. BELOW Volunteers scything the grass on Mt Halla.

In Cheju City, the best bet for those whose budget will stretch to it is probably the elegant **Cheju Grand Hotel,** which is clean and quiet and has an interesting sculpted lava rock garden. More centrally located in Cheju is the **KAL Hotel,** which has smaller rooms and somewhat lower rates than the Grand. The hotel's biggest attraction is its large casino, but during the peak periods, April-May (when the rape flowers are in bloom) and August-October, the hotel tends to become overcrowded with Japanese tour groups.

If you plan to stay in the island for several days and don't want the bother of moving hotels, you could do a lot worse than to make a beeline for Sogwip'o and use that as your base for exploring the rest of the island. With banks, shops and numerous restaurants it is quite as convenient as Cheju and a lot more restful. There are plenty of hotels and inns, too, including the **Prince Hotel,** plonked on a little island just offshore, and **Sogwip'o Lions Tourist Hotel:** the pricier hotels such as these cater predominantly for honeymooners – the **Lions Hotel,** for example, has no single rooms – so single travelers may feel more relaxed in one of the town's redoubtable *yogwan.* Several have superb views of the sea. A couple of miles to the west are the **Hyatt Regency** and other new hotels in the developing Chungmun resort area.

A popular place to spend a night, mentioned above, is **Sunrise Hotel** at the foot of Sunrise Peak in Songsanpo, at the island's eastern extreme. Staying here gives you an even chance of dragging yourself out of bed in time to scale the mountain for the day's big event (sunrise).

As is true in the rest of the country, getting around Cheju by public transport, i.e. buses, is surprisingly and blessedly simple. The only prerequisite is that you know where you want to go; if you can also decipher the destinations in *han' gul* your life will be simpler, but even if you cannot, the local people will always put you right so long as you say where you are aiming for. Buses cross and circle the island with almost incredible frequency, and there is little danger of being stranded even in the quietest hamlet.

The simplest way to get to Cheju from other parts of Korea is by air, and from Seoul, Korean Air operates 106 flights a week with a flight-time of fifty-five minutes. There are also numerous flights from Pusan, Taegu, Kwangju and Yosu. If you are coming from Japan you can fly direct to Cheju from Osaka.

The leisurely way to travel to the island is of course by sea. The car ferry which operates daily between Pusan and Cheju takes eleven-and-a-half hours. Regular passenger ferries ply daily to Cheju from Mokp'o in six hours.

THE HALLYO WATERWAY

The southern seaboard of the peninsula is the location of Korea's beautiful national sea park, the **Hallyo Waterway.** Stretching from Ch'ungmu and Hansan Island in the east to Yosu and Namhae in the west, the waterway is liberally sprinkled with islands, 115 inhabited and 253 uninhabited, which protect the waterway from the rougher seas of the Straits of Korea to the south. This region of unparalleled coastal beauty was declared a national sea park in 1968.

Pusan, far to the east, is the most popular place from which to approach the waterway, and if you are driving, the quickest way to get to it from there is to follow the Pusan-Sunchon Expressway to Masan, then take Route Two south to **Ch'ungmu** in the heart of the park. If you are not driving, the most comfortable and scenic access is by the hydrofoil which runs four times a day between Pusan and Ch'ungmu,

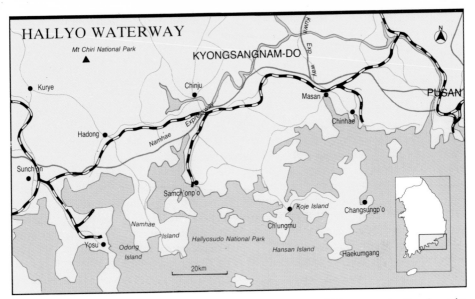

HALLYO WATERWAY

Mt Chiri National Park

KYONGSANGNAM-DO

Kurye

Chinju

Masan

Hadong

Namhae Expressway

Chinhae

PUSAN

Sunch'on

Samch'onp'o

Koje Island

Changsungp'o

Namhae

Ch'ungmu

Island

Hallyosudo National Park

Yosu

Odong Island

Hansan Island

Haekumgang

20km

covering the distance in one-and-a-half hours. Hydrofoils also connect Pusan and Yosu, as well as other points in the waterway. More details on this hydrofoil service are provided at the end of the chapter on **Pusan** (page 130-131).

If you are approaching the Hallyo Waterway after a trip down the west side of the peninsula (see **Off the Beaten Track** for details), start your southern excursion in Kwangju and follow the routes outlined in this chapter in reverse.

The charming coastal town of Ch'ungmu, which has been spared the worst of modern development, should be your principal destination in the Hallyo Waterway. From there you can reach all other places of interest. If you are coming by road from Pusan, you will pass through Chinhae and Masan, two sprawling urban ports with little of interest to the tourist, unless he happens to pass through in spring when Chinghae's cherry blossoms are a pretty sight. The Pusan-Ch'ungmu hydrofoil makes a few stops along the way at towns on the north-west coast of Koje Island, the second largest (after Cheju) of Korea's 3,300 coastal islands.

Koje Island is well worth exploring,

but it's a good idea to make it a day trip so you can get back to the comforts of Ch'ungmu by nightfall. The hydrofoil from Pusan will stop at **Changsungpo,** a tiny town which is the island's main port. From there you may hire private launches to take you around to Haekumgang, an impressive outcrop of sheer cliff which rises straight out of the blue waters of the island's southern shore. Covered with pine and camellia, this rocky bluff is one of Hallyo's "six scenic wonders." It is also a refuge for giant white herons and migrating sea birds from the southern Pacific. Excursion boats run out to Haekumgang directly from Ch'ungmu.

Ch'ungmu is an enchanting little town which gives one an excellent idea of what life all round Korea's coasts must once have been like. Few buildings are over two stories high, and what evidence there is of the twentieth century is mostly 1950s' vintage at the latest. The town is full of cozy little restaurants, second-floor cafes overlooking the streets, beer-halls and local shops. An interesting open market starts at the pier and sprawls for blocks. From the pier, ferries take tourists out sightseeing on nearby islands, and excursion boats

141

carry parties out to fish, skin-dive, and water-ski.

There are many cheap inns in the town, but for those whose budget will run to it the **Ch'ungmu Tourist Hotel** may prove irresistible. Sitting in splendid isolation on an elevated promontory, its rooms and restaurants command superb views over the entire waterway, its isles and inlets. The hotel has a nice garden for strolling in a small private beach, and its own excursion boat. There's even a disco, housed in a separate building. Along the shore just behind and below the hotel there is a row of alfresco seafood restaurants where you may eat at hand crafted burlwood tables overlooking the sea. The specialty is *sashimi*, raw fish, but they will fry it if you insist. Ignore the menu: just point out which fish or mollusks appeal to you in the tank at the entrance. A meal here may pleasantly be followed by a stroll along the paved pathway which runs the length of this pretty cove.

Ch'ungmu has several other attractions besides its natural beauty and its food. Near the Ch'ungmu Tourist Hotel is the **Yong-hwa Temple**, established by a Zen monk in 632. Destroyed and rebuilt twice, Yong-hwa-sa today is both a temple and a functioning monastery and hermitage, alive with the droning of sutras, the clanging of gongs and bells and the thumping of drums. Behind the monastery, bell-shaped tombstones mark the graves of former Buddhist masters. The walls of the shrine halls display particularly good examples of Korea's uniquely graphic form of Buddhist wall painting. If you're looking for a pleasant half-day trek in Ch'ungmu, a good hiking trail winds for three kilometers (two miles) up and around the mountain behind the temple.

On a hill overlooking downtown Ch'ungmu stands the impressive Seb-yonggwan Hall, built in 1603 to commemorate Admiral Yi's sea victory over Japan in the Imjin War of 1592-98. In fact, the whole of the Hallyo Waterway is full of reminders of Yi and his deeds. The word *"Ch'ungmu,"* for example, is derived from his posthumous title, *"ch'ung"* meaning "loyalty" and *"mu"*, martial valor. A half-hour boat ride from Ch'ungmu brings you to Hansan Island, one of the chief attractions of which is the **Chesungdang Shrine,** a complex of pavilions built by Yi and used as his naval headquarters during the Imjin War. All the buildings have been sensitively renovated in Yi dynasty style and the entire island-park is beautifully landscaped. Five large contemporary oil paintings in the shrine depict the admiral's victories. There is more Yi memorabilia en route to Hansan Island in the form of the **"Turtle Ship Lighthouse,"** a recent replica of the famous armor-plated ship.

A ferry ride due west from Ch'ungmu brings you to **Samch'onp'o,** an area dedicated to the protection of Korea's white herons, now designated as "national living treasures." You can see them congregate, long legs, sharp fishing bills, a mass of snow-white feathers, on nearby **Hakdo islet**, where they nest in the tops of tall old pine trees. Samch'onp'o is also a haven for many breeds of migratory birds from Pacific waters.

Both local ferries and the Pusan hydrofoils run across to **Yosu,** the town at the western extreme of the waterway. An expanding industrial and resort town today, Yosu also figures largely in the Admiral Yi story. The town has a full-scale replica of one of the "turtle ships," while high in the hills between City Hall and the train station is Chungmin-sa, a shrine to the admiral's memory. Those who make the steep climb to the shrine are rewarded with fine views over town and harbor.

Yosu has one tourist hotel and numerous inns near the station. The town is also an excellent area for fishing, and

RIGHT Early fall at Sorak-san National Park.

at the harbor you may hire excursion boats for fishing or sightseeing. Shuttles run from Yosu over to nearby Odong Island, which is covered with colorful camellia and is known for a special variety of bamboo from which Admiral Yi had his troops' arrows fashioned. The man follows you around in these parts!

Another shuttle connects Yosu with **Namhae,** the second largest island in the waterway after Koje. This island is linked to the mainland by a 660 m (2,165 ft)-long suspension bridge, one of the longest in the Orient.

Namhae Island's main town is also called Namhae, and from there paved roads lead to various places of interest around the island. Sangju Beach is one of the country's most beautiful and least crowded beach resorts. Mt Kumsan, famous nationwide for the quality of its sunrises, is the spot where T'aejo, the founder of the Yi dynasty, spent 100 days in prayer prior to overthrowing the Koryo dynasty.

A little inland from the waterway, and accessible from Yosu, Namhae and Samch'onp'o, is the town of Chinju, which is treated in **Off the Beaten Track.**

MT SORAK: "SNOW PEAK MOUNTAIN"

Korea is amply endowed with mountainous national parks. If you have time to visit only one, **Mt Sorak National Park,** close to the border with the North and just in from the east coast, is the obvious choice. Mt Sorak is the third highest peak in the peninsula, and the range of which it is part, T'aebaek Sanmaek, the "Great White Mountain Range," is the most spectacular in the country.

The park divides broadly into two areas, Outer and Inner Sorak. Outer Sorak, only a few minutes' drive inland from the coastal town of Sokch'o, is the more developed of the two and has comfortable hotels and inns and a variety of recreational facilities. Trails into Outer Sorak begin from the broad park just outside Sorak-dong, the little resort village in the main valley, which has a large youth hostel, numerous inns and several comfortable hotels.

144

The primary cultural attraction in Outer Sorak is the Sinhung Temple, the world's oldest surviving Zen temple, which was originally built in 652. Destroyed by forest fire, it was rebuilt in 701, then later burned down again and was restored once more in 1645. The latest renovation took place in 1971. Some of Zen Buddhism's more eccentric characters are commemorated in the temple's murals and icons. The monks Han San and Sup Duk, for example, are portrayed, grimacing grotesquely at the world from the temple's northern wall. On the rear wall of the main shrine hall, a legendary Zen aspirant is depicted presenting his amputated arm as an offering to the Zen patriarch Bodhidharma, his last-ditch attempt to persuade the great teacher that he would make a worthy disciple (Bodhidharma gave him the benefit of the doubt).

If you continue up the trail from Singhung-sa for an hour you come to the Kejo Hermitage. Built into a granite cave, it houses a beautiful golden Buddha sitting in repose amid flickering candles and burning incense. A cool, narrow stone corridor leads from the mouth of the cave into the inner sanctum. Across from the hermitage stands the famous Rolling Rock, a huge boulder apparently perched right on the edge of the cliff. With considerable effort you may set this rock a'rolling, but you'll never roll it off the cliff. From here trails wind even further up toward the granite peaks; if you have the strength, make for Ulsanbawi Rock, a craggy outcrop of granite 650 m (2,145 ft) high, with breathtaking views of Sorak below and the East Sea in the distance.

Another hour's walk beyond Flying Fairy Peak brings you to Kumgang Cave and its terrific views. Another trail from the peak leads across a swaying suspension bridge over a narrow gorge to Flying Dragon Waterfall.

Three upper-range hotels in Outer Sorak which may be recommended are Sorak Park Hotel, Mt Sorak Tourist Hotel and New Sorak Hotel, but there is plenty of simple accommodation available, too.

Inner Sorak remains relatively un-

OPPOSITE AND ABOVE Sorak-san National Park is Korea's most scenic. Excellent recreational facilities and accommodation abound making a visit a rewarding experience.

developed and hence attracts more experienced trekkers and climbers, not to mention those who want to get away from the crowds: Outer Sorak can seem a mite too popular when swarming with school-kids and students. Trails here are less well marked than in Outer Sorak, and anyone who fancies tackling them is advised to buy a detailed large scale map of the area before leaving Seoul.

There are a number of ways of approaching Inner Sorak. From the park beyond Sorak-dong you may take the cable car to Kwongumsong and from here trails connect directly to Inner Sorak. Coming from Seoul, the best approach is along the Han River to Inje. From Inje there are two routes into the Sorak range: the northern route, which passes the Chingpuryong and the Misilfrom the roadside rest-stop called Chang-sudae Villa, and the **Paekdam Temple**, a considerably longer and more difficult climb along the same trail. Further down the road towards the coast is another trail which leads up to the **Yongdam Waterfall**, the **Pongjong-Am Hermitage** and **Taechong-bong Peak**, at 1,708 meters the highest peak in the Sorak range. Be prepared for an arduous four to six-hour trek up steep, twisting trails if you choose this hike; wear appropriate clothes and boots and bring along water and snacks, for here you will find few signs of civilization. Before reaching Yangyang, where marvelous seafood awaits the deserving hiker, stop off at the **Osaek Yaksu Mineral Springs** for a soothing hot soak.

Sorak is the most scenic mountain park in Korea, and one of the best in the world. A delicate balance has been struck between development and conservation; artificial structures and materials have been kept to a minimum, and all construction is undertaken with taste and consideration for the environment. A five square kilometer (two square mile) park called "Leisure Land East" is currently under construction on a coastal stretch of the park, so let's hope that these standards will be equally evident there, too. Facilities in the park will include camping grounds, hot-spring spas, ski slopes, hunting, fishing, water-skiing, tennis, golf and indoor sports.

The fastest way to Sorak is by plane. The flight from Seoul to Sokch'o takes forty minutes, and the bus-or cab-ride from there to Sorak-dong another half hour. Eighteen buses a day run between Sokch'o and Seoul, and the one-way journey takes five hours. Buses travel to Sokch'o along the Yongdong Expressway to the coast at Kangnung, and this is also the quickest route to follow if you are traveling into the area by car.

ryong Passes and terminates at **Sokch'o**, is the roughest and most remote; the southern route through the Hangyeryong Pass takes you to the coastal town of Yangyang, and this is the most scenic and convenient way to approach the area from inland.

Favorite sights along this southern route to Inner Sorak include the **Taesung Falls,** an easy hike up the trail

LEFT "Snow Peak Mountain" cable car glides through Sorak-san National Park.

Korea: Off the Beaten Track

The destinations described in **The Broad Highway**, above, are those places which are so special historically, culturally or scenically that they demand to be seen by every visitor to Korea who can possibly spare the time. If you haven't seen Kyongju, for example, a vital wedge of the peninsula's history remains unknown to you; if you haven't traveled around Cheju Island, you've missed one of East Asia's most charming and balmy experiences.

Korea has many other places, however, which, though not unmissable in this way, have a lot to offer the traveler who is in the country for a rather more extended stay. What follows is our selection of the best of these.

AROUND SEOUL

INCH'ON

The traditional entranceway to the country for foreigners, **Inch'on** is Korea's fourth largest city and third busiest port. Long an important conduit for trade with China, it also became host to the first Western diplomatic and trade missions after the signing of the Korean-American Treaty of Amity and Commerce in 1882.

Inch'on earned another paragraph in the history books on September 15, 1950 when it was the site of General Douglas MacArthur's daring pre-dawn amphibious landing, a coup which turned the tide of the Korean War. After twelve days of bloody fighting, this landing led to the recapture of Seoul from Communist forces. In commemoration of the event, a 10 m (33 ft) high statue of the general stands at the peak of Freedom Hill, looking over the Yellow Sea.

Today Inch'on is a busy shipping and industrial town with relatively few historical sites of interest to the tourist. Nearby are the beaches of **Song-do**, which are always crowded during the summer, but if you have time you can take a ferry across to some of the remoter outer islands, or down the west coast, where you will find cleaner, less crowded beaches and pleasant lagoons.

Perhaps Inch'on's greatest attraction is the excellent seafood served in rustic restaurants on some of the nearby land-linked islands such as **Wolmi** and **Sowolmi**.

Inch'on has a major deluxe hotel, the **Olympus**, with 200 rooms, a nightclub, a casino, a large swimming pool and both Korean and Western restaurants. Local inns offer less expensive and more traditional accommodation. If you're traveling by car, the expressway will take you from Seoul to Inch'on in less than thirty minutes.

NORTH AND SOUTH HAN FORTRESSES

There are two major fortresses in the Seoul area which date back two thousand years. **Pukhansansong** (the Northern) and **Namhansansong** (the Southern) were both constructed in the early Paekche period, after which they fell into disuse. Yi kings restored them during the seventeenth century under threat of invasion by the Manchus.

The northern fortress is located to the northeast of Seoul and skirts the ridges of Pukhan (Northern Han) Mountain. With this historic site as a backdrop, the surrounding forests and meadows are popular for hiking and picnics.

Thirty kilometers (18 miles) southeast of Seoul, the walls and seventeen gates of the southern fortress snake for eight kilometers (five miles) along Namhan (Southern Han) Mountain. This impressive fortification, which stands over twenty feet high in places, is the more popular of the two. It was here in 1636 that King Injo finally surrendered to invading Manchu forces. On a clear day the summit provides spectacular views of the Han River Valley.

The fortress is just east of Songnam. Reach it through Songnam, off the Seoul-Pusan Expressway, or from National Route 3 on the way to Kwangju.

ROYAL TOMBS

Royal burial grounds are among Korea's most tranquil and scenic settings, and there are numerous such parks in the Seoul area. The underground chambers are covered over with round mounds of earth and domed with layers of green turf, marked with simple but elegant stone shrines and set among groves of pine or bamboo.

At **Kumgok**, about forty minutes north east of Seoul by car, lie the **Hong Yurung Tombs**, the graves of Korea's last two kings, Kojong and Sonjong, and their wives. Set in a wooded park full of magpies, orioles and cuckoos, these classical Korean burial mounds are perfect examples of the tranquil, naturally landscaped settings preferred by Korean kings for their resting-places. The white stone guardians, which include representations of war-riors, scholars and mythical animals from the Oriental zodiac, look like smaller versions of the giant stone statues which keep vigil over the route to the Ming imperial tombs north of Peking.

Near Kumgok is **Tonggu-Rung**, where King T'aejo, founder of the Yi dynasty, was buried in 1408. A little further north at **Kwangnung**, 28 km (17 miles) outside Seoul, is the most delightful of these parks in the Seoul area: the burial ground of King Sejo (died 1468) and his wife Queen Yum Chon-hi. These magnificent mounds lie deep in thick forests, as does **Pongson Temple**, which was recently renovated in traditional style.

More burial parks are to be found just beyond the south-eastern suburbs of Seoul. **Honnhung** contains the tomb of King T'aejong (1367-1422) and Queen Wonkyong, and **Innung** contains the tombs of King Sunjo (1790-1834) and Queen Sunwon. These parks are located in the fertile farmbelt re-

ABOVE Fish dock at Inch'on, the major port west of Seoul which is also Korea's fourth largest city.

151

nowned for its juicy melons and strawberries, fruits which are served in little stalls here during spring and summer.

SONGNI NATIONAL PARK

Songni means "escape from the vulgar" – ironic in view of the fact that the greatest attraction of this area is the remarkably vulgar 88-foot high concrete Buddha at Popju Temple, the biggest Buddha in Korea. This mountainous area does, however, offer fine opportunities for escaping the city and its fumes, and it's only

dong is the starting-point for hikes up around the 22 temples and pavilions which are scattered among Mt Sogni's craggy peaks and wooded valleys. The village also has a tourist hotel and several *yogwan* for those who feel like exploring the area thoroughly.

Songni's best-known attraction is **Popju-sa,** a temple founded in 553. Formerly this was one of the greatest temples in the land, and there are numerous relics from its days of glory preserved in the grounds. The gigantic Miruk (Buddha of the Future) makes up

three hours by car from Seoul. If you're going by public transport take a train or express bus to Taechon, then transfer to local bus or taxi for the ride up to the mountain.

After leaving the expressway and passing through the town of Ch'ongju, you enter the winding **Malti Pass,** which leads up to Mt Songni's summit.

The mountain village of **Songni-**

The temple buildings of Chikchi-sa ABOVE near Taejon City in central Korea date back to the sixteenth century but the temple was founded much earlier.

in size for what it lacks in years: it was completed in 1964. If time and energy permit, trek along some of Sogni's excellent hiking trails up to the ridges above the Popju Temple, which offer great views of the temple complex and surrounding landscape.

SANJONG LAKE

North-east of Seoul, just beyond the town of Uijongbu, is an artificial lake resort built by the Japanese during their occupation of the peninsula. It's called

Sanjong Lake, and North Korean dictator Kim Il-sung maintained a summer villa here prior to the Korean War, when the area lay within northern jurisdiction. Today Sanjong Lake is very popular for hiking and picnics in summer and skating in winter.

En route to or from Sanjong Lake, you might like to stop at the Chongnung Valley, a popular picnic and hiking area on the northern outskirts of Seoul, near the Pugak Skyway. Here you'll find Kyongguk Temple, perhaps the most beautifully landscaped temple complex in the Seoul area.

The road north to Sanjong Lake also takes you through a broad pass between two of Seoul's most popular mountains for hiking: Mt Tobang to the west, rough and rocky, and the more rounded Mt Surak to the east. Easily reached from Seoul, both mountains are riddled with well-worn hiking trails and dotted with the ruins of ancient hermitages.

HAN RIVER LAKE RESORTS

About an hour and a half north-east of Seoul is Korea's most scenic lake country. The north-east province of Kangwon-do is a land of misty mountains, lakes, meandering rivers, and fertile valleys neatly sculpted into green rice paddies and vegetable patches. The lakes created by the Soyang and Paltang dams provide the setting for pleasant resorts which have become favorite holiday destinations for Seoul's teeming millions. They also make ideal countryside retreats for travelers with limited time in Korea, or a brief interlude for those on the way to the mountains of Mt Sorak National Park (see The Broad Highway).

A good place to spend a night or two before reaching Ch'unch'on is Namisom Island, set in the middle of the Han River, about an hour's drive out of Seoul. There you can rent a cozy bungalow and relax among the whispering pines and placid waters. Ferryboats run regularly between the shore and the island.

Twenty miles further north lies Ch'unch'on, and the most attractive way to get there is by riverboat. Ch'unch'on Lake and the other waters nearby constitute Korea's best lake resort country, with facilities for fishing, swimming, sailing and water-skiing. In Ch'unch'on look out for Ethiopia House, a Korean tea-house with good views over the lake; and the Koryo Silk Factory, where you may watch the silk

being made.

There are other worthwhile resorts beyond Ch'unch'on. Due north of Samyong Mountain, near Hwachon, is Paro Lake, which is usually less crowded than Ch'unch'on's. But the most scenic of all Korea's inland waterways is Soyang Lake, created by the waters of the Soyang Dam. Tours of the lake are offered from the pier known as Soyang Pavilion.

ABOVE Interior of Chikchi Temple which houses the 1,000 Buddhas for which it is famous. Chikchi-sa is halfway between Taegu and Taejon.

An interesting side-trip from Soyang Lake entails a 15- minute boat ride north from Soyang pavilion and a 20-minute hike up a steep hillside from the dock. After passing a waterfall, you will stumble upon **Chongp'yong Temple,** a Buddhist retreat founded 1,600 years ago. The temple has especially fine murals on its exterior walls.

Even more remote is the town of **Yanggu,** northeast of Soyang, about a one-and-a-half-hour boat ride from the Soyang Pavilion. The town, accessible from the dock by bus or taxi, is in a secluded valley only a few miles from the DMZ. Yanggu is a typical Korean country town, shut off from most Western influences. There are inns where you can put up if you feel like drinking in the atmosphere at your leisure. Yanggu is as far as you can go in the lake country by boat.

From Yanggu you are within striking distance of Inje, inland gateway to Mt Sorak National Park. See **The Broad Highway** for details.

THE EAST SIDE: COAST RESORTS AND MOUNTAIN RETREATS

Stretching 390 km (242 miles) from Hwajinpo Beach just below the DMZ down to the industrial city of P'ohang, Korea's east coast has the country's most spectacular seascapes. A region of many contrasts, the rugged coastline is punctuated by deep ravines and prominent pine bluffs, quiet fishing coves and pretty inland lagoons. The clear blue water and clean white sand make for some of Korea's best swimming beaches. Wooded promontories with old pavilions are found along the entire length of the coast, while only minutes' inland are scenic mountain parks and relaxing hot spring spas.

To reach the coast from Seoul take the Yongdong Expressway from Seoul to Kangnung. About half an hour before Kangnung on the southern side of the expressway is the **Dragon Valley Ski Resort,** Korea's best, eight kilometers (five miles) from the expressway. The resort has three slopes, all equipped with chair-lifts, equipment rental stores, lights for night skiing and so on.

At Kangnung, terminus of the expressway, turn north on to the coast road and head for **Sokch'o.** This major fishing port has excellent fish restaurants and is only 15 minutes from Mt Sorak National Park. Just outside the town is the new **Choksan Hot Springs Resort;** to the north is **Hwajinpo Beach,** one of Korea's best beach resorts, where many of Seoul's wealthy maintain villas.

Heading south again, but before Yangyang, is **Naksan Temple,** which dates from 671. A fifteenth century bell and a Koryo dynasty pagoda are among its treasures, but the most famous feature here is the 16 m (52 ft) white granite staue of Kuan Yi, the goddess of mercy.

Drive through Yangyang and continue down the coast until you see the sign for **Hajodae Pavilion.** Located on a beautiful pine- covered promontory, the pavilion offers superb views of the eastern coastline. Nearby is **Hajodae Beach,** another good place to stop for a swim.

Continuing south, you'll soon see the sign for **Mt Odae National Park,** pointing inland. The region around 1,563 m (5,128 ft) high Mt Odae is dotted with old hermitages, meditation retreats and Shilla era artifacts. There are also two famous temples, **Woljong-sa** and **Sangwon-sa.**

At Woljong Temple, in the southern part of this mountain park, you'll see a fine nine-story pagoda, octagonal in shape, capped by a sculpted lotus and a bronze pinnacle. Woljong's other unusual attraction is a sculpture of a kneeling Buddha, also located in front of the main hall.

Sangwon Temple, situated east of

the main peak and higher up than Woljong, boasts the oldest and second largest bell in the country, cast in 725. Like Woljong, this temple was founded by the monk Chajang, during the Shilla era.

Kangnung is a quiet fishing resort which comes to life each spring on the fifth day of the fifth month by the lunar calendar (usually in June) for its weeklong **Tano Spring Festival.** The main attraction hereabouts for visitors is the **Kyongp'odae Beach Resort,** a few kilometers to the north, which has inns, from Kangnung early in the morning.

Just south of Kangnung is the **Jugseo-ru Pavilion,** a thirteenth century pleasure pavilion which was the setting for aristocratic moon-gazing parties.

As soon as you pass the exits for Uljin, look out for the sign to the **Sugryu Limestone Cave.** It's in a park by a reservoir a few kilometers inland, a 470 m (1,542 ft) cave formed over 250 million years ago. Its insides are covered with odd-looking stalactites, stalagmites and other rock formations. The juniper tree growing by the cave's

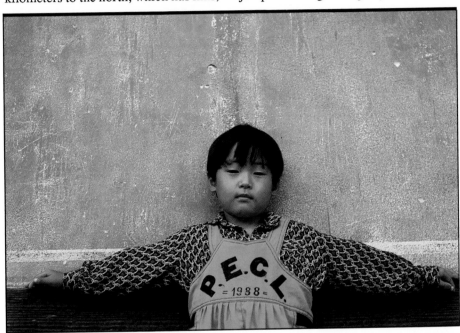

hotels and good seafood restaurants as well as a very decent beach.

From Kangnung the drive south used to be quite rough, but recently the whole stretch has been graded and paved and nowadays this section of the coast is reminiscent of California's Highway One between Monterey and Big Sur, with its fabulous shorelines and rugged mountains dropping abruptly to the sea. Allowing plenty of time for leisurely stops along the way, the drive to P'ohang, where the coast road ends, takes about a day, so it's best to set out

entrance is allegedly 1,000 years old, an appropriate sort of age for this favorite symbol of longevity.

Health enthusiasts will enjoy a stop at **Paekam Mineral Springs,** 40 km (25 miles) south of Uljin and 10 km (6 miles) inland. Constructed in traditional style, this large new building houses two enormous bath complexes, one for

ABOVE Boy at Popju-sa Temple wearing a chain-link vest and a reminder of the year Koreans cannot allow themselves to forget.

each sex. The bathrooms are clean and spacious, and the hot and cold pools most invigorating.

The next spot of interest en route to P'ohang is **Mt. Chuwang National Park**, reached via the coastal town of Yongdog, which incidentally is famous for its "Yongdog Crab." Chuwang is a range of tall granite peaks and deep gorges, an ideal place to lose yourself for a spell, if that's what you feel like doing. Visitors here are infrequent.

Halfway between Yongdog and P'ohang is **Pogyong Temple**, founded in the Shilla era and surrounded by magnificent mountain scenery. A short hike will bring you to a cool pool formed by one of the eleven waterfalls in the area, a great place for a refreshing summer dip. A pleasant local inn provides comfortable accommodation for those who choose to break their journey here.

There's no mistaking **P'ohang**, some 25 km (15 miles) south of Pogyong-sa - the city's chimneys stain the sky yellow and gray with fumes. A port as well as one of Korea's most important centers of heavy industry, P'ohang's pride and joy is the P'ohang Iron and Steel Company, Korea's first integrated steel mill, which rolls out some eight million tons of crude steel every year.

The best reason for stopping in P'ohang is to catch the Han Il Ho express ferry to Ullung Island, six hours and 268 km (166 miles) out into the East Sea.

ULLUNG ISLAND

Ullung is one of Korea's least-known yet most charming destinations. **To-dong**, the main town on the south east coast where the ferry docks, retains a rustic air with simple, functional dwellings. There are many good *yogwan* in

ABOVE Wall painting of patriarch in sub-temple of Haein-sa Temple, near Taegu.

the town, and the ones along To-dong Harbor provide superb views of the sea and the fishing boats from rooftop patios. You'll notice that many doors in Ullung have no locks: among other things, the island is known for its absolute freedom from crime.

The island has lots of pleasant walks. **Songinbong**, at 984 m (3,228 ft) the island's highest peak, requires about half a day to hike up and back and there are good views from the top of the island and the surrounding sea. The paved road which circles the island is of recent date. You may take a taxi in To-dong for a round-the-island tour, or walk it instead. The 40 km (25 mile) hike takes about three days.

The island and its neighbor, **Chuk**, may also be profitably explored by boat. Two of the best beaches, are **Watari**, on the east coast, where a waterfall splashes down into a saltwater pool, and **Satekam Beach**, a cove with warm, unruffled waters, ideal for swimming.

Off Ullung's east coast sits **Chuk**, a surprisingly productive little island easily reached by boat. A hard hike brings you to the island's flattened top, where there is a farm of pampered, corn-fed stock which produces some of Korea's best beef. New calves from the mainland are carried bodily up the slope to the farm, and when they have been fattened they are lowered by rope and pulley to barges below. Chuk-do also produces watermelons, bamboo, and mulberry leaves for silkworm production, while the harvest of sea fruits brought to the surfaace by the diving women of Ullung includes lobsters, crabs, abalone and sea cucumbers.

Unlike the even remoter but much larger Cheju Island, Ullung has very little tourist infrastructure, and its attractions for the visitor, as this account suggests, aré fairly low-key. As an island escape, however, it probably has no equal in the peninsula.

ANDONG AND HAHOE

Due to the depredations of Korea's successive conquerors, the places where traditional Korea survives in its best and purest form are those that are relatively hard to get to – places that the Mongols, the Japanese and the Manchus all failed to reach. One of the most remarkable of these is the village of Hahoe. The nearest town to **Hahoe** is Andong, an interesting spot in its own right, and from Andong a number of other curious survivors can be reached. Some 60 miles from the east coast, Andong is accessible by bus from Taegu to the south or Yongdog on the coast.

Andong is the ancestral home of the Kwon clan, an important *yangban* (aristocrat) family which held many high government posts during the Yi dynasty. Although the center has been modernized in tawdry fashion, large old dwellings of the gentry survive in the town, and they give an excellent idea of the old *yangban* way of life.

On the outskirts of the town on the east side stands what is often referred to as the oldest and biggest pagoda in Korea. Seven stories high, the brick structure is engraved with images of temple guardians and Deva kings, and dates from the United Shilla era. Close by is the well-preserved residence of a local nobleman. A little further on in the same direction, on the shore of a recently-created dam lake, is an artificial village of traditional houses which were moved here to prevent their being inundated. The houses range from simple thatched cottages to inns for the accommodation of official envoys and the elaborate tiled villa of an aristocrat. Like the folk village at Suwon, near Seoul, the atmosphere is much more authentic than one would expect – especially at the inns, where *makkolli* and *anju* are served and supped just as in the old days. One curious relic is a stone ice-house, where sweetfish, a local product presented to the king as tribute, were stored.

Other attractions in the vicinity of Andong include the **Pongjong Temple,** 16 km (10 miles) to the northwest, and a 12 m (39 ft) **Amita Buddha** carved into an enormous granite boulder, located five kilometers (three miles) north along Route 5. On a pine-covered hill behind this massive image of Buddha stands another old pagoda. Both date from the Koryo dynasty.

Twenty-eight kilometers (17 miles) north of Andong is the **Tosan Sowon Confucian Academy,** a typical institute of higher learning in the days of neo-Confucian orthodoxy. It was established by Yi Whang, Korea's foremost Confucian scholar, during the late sixteenth century. Though no longer in use, the buildings and some of the artifacts they contain are well preserved. The architectural style characteristic of schools such as this, which differs substantially from that used for schools and palaces, is a rare sight in Korea today.

And so to the little hamlet of **Hahoe,**

even more remote and quintessentially Korean than Andong, from which it is a half-hour drive to the south-west. The last stretch is slow, winding and bumpy as the road is unpaved.

"*Hahoe*" means "enfolded by the river," which the village is, and it's this feature, reinforced by the mountains which lie beyond the river, that has allowed the village to survive successive wars and invasions unscathed. The oldest house in Hahoe has been here for more than 530 years; the family of the gentleman who runs the tiny village

store has lived here for twenty generations, some 600 years. The only modern building is the school, and the government has now come round to the view that Hahoe's archaic appearance deserves to be maintained. All new structures in the village are now being built in the old way, and thatch is used for the roofs, even though it has been eliminated from most parts of the country in the effort to give Korea a bright modern image.

Hahoe is much like the folk villages of Suwon or Andong, with two important differences: there is nothing artificial about the place, so not only the buildings themselves but also the way they are arranged reflect age-old social realities; and visitors are not so much welcomed as suffered, for the traditions of Hahoe are proud and aristocratic. Use discretion and common sense as you poke around, remembering that people really live here.

PUSOK TEMPLE

Pusok-sa ("Floating Rock Temple") is one of the most inaccessible in the country. Like Hahoe, it is so remote that the Japanese never found it during their sixteenth century rampage through the country. Consequently, Pusok-sa has some of Korea's oldest temple buildings and Buddhist artifacts. About 60 km (37 miles) north of Andong along Route 5, it's a long, bumpy ride along dusty, unpaved roads, but for the intrepid and for students of Buddhism the effort is well rewarded.

The temple was established in 676 by the great Shilla priest Uisang, after his return from China. During his youth, Uisang fell in love with a beautiful girl named Myohwa ("Delicate Flower"), but before he could marry her she was whisked away by court officials and sent as a gift to a T'ang emperor of China. Heart-broken, Uisang entered the priesthood, and ultimately became one of Korea's greatest holy men. During his pilgrimage to China he again crossed paths with Myohwa, whose devotion to him remained so strong that her spirit followed his boat back to Korea and transformed itself into an enormous boulder to protect him and his new temple from the thieves which infested the area. This "floating rock" still balances precariously

ABOVE Ancient wattle-and-daub houses in the remote village of Hahoe, where very little has changed since the days of the Yi. OPPOSITE Pagoda of Popju-sa Temple, in Mt Songni National Park.

outside the main hall.

Later, according to the legend, Myohwa took the form of a stone dragon, which burrowed beneath the temple until its head was at the altar and its tail 18 m (60 ft) away by the lantern. Just another tall Buddhist story? So you might well suppose, but several years ago a team of scientists down from Seoul to study the temple scientifically excavated an area near the lantern in front of the main hall, and soon uncovered part of a large stone formation shaped like a dragon's tail. It even had scale-like patterns etched on it. After that they decided to let sleeping dragons lie.

The main hall, **Muryangsu-jon** (**"Hall of Eternal Life"**), dates from the mid-fourteenth century and is the oldest surviving wooden structure in Korea. Its unusual tapered columns are said to reflect Greek influence. Also from the Koryo period is the nine-foot seated figure of **Amita Buddha**. Made entirely of clay, coated with lacquer and gilt, it is the only icon of its kind in Korea. Pusok-sa's **Koryo wall paintings**, designated as national treasures, are the oldest such paintings in the country.

THE WEST SIDE: MOUNTAINS, TEMPLES, AND THE PAEKCHE LEGACY

While Korea's east coast is known principally for its beautiful sea shores and maritime scenery, the West side is famous for its relics of the Paekche Kingdom, which held sway over the western plains and coast from near the beginning of the Christian era until its defeat by the combined forces of T'ang China and Shilla in 660. As in Kyongju, though less dramatically, recent archaeological finds have helped to bring this remote period in the region's history back to life.

The west of the peninsula also has marvelous mountain parks dotted with weather-beaten old temples, but until recently it has been much less oriented toward tourism than other parts of the country. The unearthing of the Paekche artifacts - and growing recognition by the authorities of the usefulness of tourist dollars - has resulted in a new emphasis being placed on the reconstruction of historical sites, especially around the old capital cities of Puyo and Kongju.

A good place to begin your west side tour is at the popular hot-spring resort of **Onyang**, less than an hour's drive south of Seoul. To get there, take the Seoul-Pusan Expressway south as far as Chonan, then exit west onto Highway 21, and follow the road 18 km (11 miles) out to Onyang.

Onyang is a pleasant resort-town popular among honeymooners without the time or money to go further afield. It has many hotels and inns, all of which are equipped with natural hot-spring baths. There's enough to do and see in Onyang to justify an overnight stay, but even if you are just passing through it's worth stopping for a mineral bath and a massage.

Since 1978, Onyang's main attraction has been the **Onyang Folk Museum**, privately built and owned by one Kim Won-dae. His collection of 7,000 folk artifacts may well be the best of its type in the country.

The other thing Onyang is famous for is the **Hyonch'ung-sa Shrine**, an extensive memorial park dedicated to the naval hero Admiral Yi, who was born and raised here. First erected by King Sukchong in 1704, it fell into disrepair during the Japanese occupation. It was re-opened by President Park on 28 April 1969, the anniversary of the admiral's birth, which is now celebrated here annually with a colorful festival.

The shrine itself sits high on a hillside overlooking the park, one of the prettiest in Korea. There is also a museum of relics, the tomb of his favorite son, who died defending the family home against the Japanese, and a large artificial lotus pond.

BEACHES AND FLOWERS

From Onyang head westward into the Kaya Hills toward Sosan, gateway to the T'ae-an Peninsula. Halfway there you'll find the **Sudok Temple** perched high on the southern slope of Mt Toksung. A rather arduous climb above this temple brings you to a large **Maitreya Buddha** carved into the face of the mountain.

Due west from Sosan is the town of **T'ae-an,** the last major bus terminus for this portion of the west coast. From T'ae-an you are within easy reach of three beaches and a scenic island, all of which are part of the **Sosan Seashore National Park.** To the south is Anmyon Island, a beautiful island covered with unusual flora. Between T'ae-an and Amnyon is **Mallipo Beach,** one of Korea's finest swimming resorts, with comfortable lodging facilities and over two miles of clean sandy beach.

A little to the north of Mallipo lies **Chollipo Beach,** a haven for for fanciers of exotic flora. Here you'll find the **Chollipo Arboretum,** a project initiated in 1970 by Carl Ferris Miller, a long-time American resident of Korea and now a Korean citizen. Over 6,000 domestic and imported species are cultivated here, including the rarest members of the magnolia family and the world's best collection of ilex. People with a serious interest in unusual flora are welcome to pay a visit.

On the coast just below Amnyon Island is one of Seoul's favorite beach resorts, **Taechon Beach,** 14 km (9 miles) from the town of Taechon in the middle of one of Korea's lushest agricultural basins.

Taechon's broad, clean beach is divided, albeit vaguely, between a "Korean beach" to the north and a "Foreigners' beach" to the south. The Korean beach is backed by a number of little inns and eateries and remains lively day and night during the summer. The foreigners' end is considerably more peaceful. Missionary families were the first foreigners to discover the resort, but these days villas and bungalows are maintained here by international businessmen and bankers as well, who find it to be well within weekend fleeing distance from Seoul. Visitors may arrange to rent one of theese houses by inquiring in the town.

PUYO AND KONGJU: PAEKCHE CAPITALS

Kongju was the capital of the Paekche kingdom between 475 and 538. In 1971, workers digging a drainage ditch just outside this modest provincial educational center and market town stumbled on an incredible find: the tomb of a Paekche king – totally undisturbed since the sixth century. It was the **Tomb of King Muryong,** who ruled between 501 and 523, and it was found to contain over 3,000 invaluable artifacts. This brick-lined tomb and others nearby are open for inspection some 15 minutes on foot north-east of the town center. A selection of the treasures discovered – pots, gold and silver jewelry, extraordinarily long ornamental shoes of bronze – are displayed at **Kongju National Museum,** in the middle of the town.

The other things worth knowing about Kongju are the steep, wooded **San Sung Dong Park** which crowds down almost into the town center, and the annual festival, featuring fireworks, a parade and traditional dancing, which falls in mid-October.

Hidden deep in mountains about 25 km (15 miles) north of Kongju, surrounded by wooded hills, streams and convoluted rock formations, is an ancient temple called **Magok-sa,** one of those places that time forgot. The temple was founded in the Shilla period by the aristocratic priest who also founded T'ongdo-sa, Korea's largest temple. The central courtyard has a fine five-story Koryo period pagoda while an 80-foot Bodhi Tree, like the one under which the Buddha attained enlightenment, shades one side of the courtyard.

Fifty kilometers (30 miles) southwest of Kongju along Highway 23 lies **Puyo,** Paekche's second capital. Rich in legends and relics, Puyo is rapidly becoming a major tourist destination. The **Puyo National Museum** houses prehistoric implements found in the area, as well as artifacts from Paekche times.

In a spacious park set on a steep hill in the middle of Puyo is the site where the last king of Paekche made his final stand against invading armies from T'ang China. Among the many pavilions and historical relics preserved in this park, the most dramatic sight is **Falling Flowers Cliff,** a steep and rocky promontory overlooking White Horse River. As the story goes, the Chinese general Su Ting-fang, on the far side of the river, was poised to make his final assault on Paekche when 3,000 palace ladies in full regalia hurled themselves en masse from the cliff into the river, preferring death to dishonor at the hands of foreign soldiers. As they fell their colorful skirts billowed out around them, suggesting the image of falling flowers. A pavilion in their honor stands at the top of the cliff.

Facing west in this melancholy park is the **Songwoldae** or **Moon-gazing Pavilion,** where the last Paekche king kept vigil on the night before his final battle; facing east is the **Yongilru** or **Sun-greeting Pavilion,** where he witnessed what he knew would be his last sunrise. Further down the hill you'll find the **Samching-sa Shrine,** erected in

honor of three great Paekche heroes. A colorful ceremony is held at this shrine every October, during the town's annual Paekche Culture Festival.

The town of Puyo itself is pleasant and quiet, with an interesting maze of lanes in the center where markets, restaurants and taverns are located. The place to stay is the relatively new **Puyo Youth Hostel.** Don't be misled by the name, for in addition to dormitory facilities for youngsters, the "hostel" has comfortable private rooms for tourists, a coffee-shop and even a swimming pool. The White Horse River flows a little way down the street from here, while the hilltop park is just behind the hostel.

Southwest of Puyo along Highway 23 is the nondescript town of Nonsan, outside which is **Kwanchog (Candlelight) Temple** and its far from nondescript **Unjin Miruk, Buddha of the Future,** the largest stone Buddha in the country. This is something to see, even if it requires a diversion, with its broad and flat but strangely intellectual face and its huge, two-tiered tray-like headdress pressed up against the dense woods behind the temple. Though carved by a relatively unskilled local craftsman 1,000 years ago, the image has a rivetingly attractive and mysterious quality. Kwanchog Temple also has a fine five-story pagoda and a large stone lantern, both as old as the statue.

If you can spare a few days to explore the area around Kongju and Puyo, a hike in the mountains of **Kyeryong-san National Park** is highly recommended. Two of the most popular entrances to the park are punctuated by beautiful old temples, Kap-sa and Tonghak-sa respectively, and the steep climb in between, following the prancing course of a mountain stream for

OPPOSITE Faces from the Korean countryside. Thatched cottages of the type seen TOP have almost disappeared, victims of the government's determination to give Korea a modern image. This specimen is from the Folk Village at Suwon.

much of the way, is exhilarating.

Halfway between Taejon and Kwangju, 93 km (58 miles) south of Seoul, is the quaint town of **Chonju**, ancestral home of the Yi clan, which founded Korea's last dynasty in 1392. Today it is most famous for its food and paper. Paper was introduced into Korea from China about a thousand years ago, and the craftsmen of Chonju still employ traditional methods and materials to manufacture some of the finest paper in the Orient. Raw materials include mulberry, bamboo, bark chips and even algae.

Chonju is also one of Korea's great culinary centers, and the local *pièce de resistance* is a dish called *pipimpap*, a large bowl of rice topped with bean sprouts, broiled beef, poached squid, mountain vegetables, roasted sesame seeds, pine nuts and an egg. It comes with a rich beef broth and half a dozen types of kimch'i. You can try this marvelous dish at the **Han Il Kwan Restaurant**, an old establishment with an excellent reputation nationwide.

While in Chonju you may like to visit one of Korea's finest private antique shop-cum-museums, the **Chon Bok Tuk San Pun Chon**, which has Shilla ceramics, traditional folk masks, antique jewelry and much more.

TEMPLES AND MOUNTAIN PARKS

Numerous interesting side-trips are possible from Chonju. En route to Mt. Mai is **Songwang Temple**, the walls and ceilings of which are covered with some of Korea's most colorful Buddhist murals. Of relatively recent origin, they anticipate contemporary graphic art and animated cartoons in style.

Mt Mai means "Horse Ears Mountain" and is so called because its two peaks resemble this when seen from the north at Chinan village. Hike up to Hwaom Cave through the Chonghwang Pass, then continue along the trail until

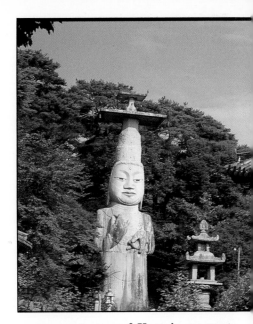

you come to one of Korea's most extraordinary religious sites, the **T'ap-sa** or "**Pagoda temple**." An eccentric hermit named Yi Kap-yong spent a lifetime piling up thousands of dry stones to form dozens of crude "shaking pagodas," ranging in height from a few centimeters to ten meters (30 ft). Incredibly, many of them have survived centuries of weather and warfare. T'ap-sa is not a Buddhist temple, but rather a shrine to the hermit Yi's own personal religion, his own brand of animism. The paths beyond his "shaking pagodas" lead to several more orthodox temples nearby. You will probably find yourself looking at them with new eyes.

North-east of Chonju, beyond Mt Mai, is **Mt Tokyu National Park**, located on the old fortified frontier which separated the three ancient kingdoms of Koguryo, Shilla and Paekche. At **Mt Mudok** there are several good inns, and nearby is the **Paekryong Temple**. Deeper into the mountains are steep slopes which provide an attractive challenge for serious climbers.

Thirty-two kilometers (20 miles) southwest of Chonju, surrounded by those who wish to spend an extra day hiking in these mountains. In autumn Mt Naejang is a great alternative to the parks closer to Seoul for those allergic to crowds.

KWANGJU: FOOD, WINE, TEA

The city of **Kwangju**, final stop before the south coast, is an hour's drive south of Paegyang Temple. On the way is the village of **Tamyang**, where mats, baskets, chopsticks and other items are fashioned from bamboo.

Kwangju is the hometown of former presidential candidate Kim Dae-jung and the heart of democratic opposition to the present regime. When Kim was arrested in 1980 his supporters in Kwangju took to the streets in angry protest; the resulting confrontation with the army, which left some 190 people dead, cast a shadow over Korean politics which has yet to lift. Kwangju people frequently suffer discrimination from other Koreans, and visitors may pick up on the political atmosphere in the town, which is never far below simmering.

Like Chonju, Kwangju is famous for food, and the connoisseur would be hard pressed to decide which of the two offers superior fare. The fertile Honam basin provides the abundant and varied ingredients required to continue a great gourmet tradition started here centuries ago by the region's noblemen. Kwangju also produces some of the best Korean liquor, notably *chungchong* (barley and rice wine) and *makkolli*.

Kwangju's tea is noted nationwide, notably the "Early Spring Tea." The tender green leaves used for this delicious brew are cultivated and picked in the mountains nearby by monks, then steamed and dried nine times in a long

the wooded slopes of Mt Moak, sits **Kumsan ("Gold Mountain") Temple**, which, with its three-story Miruk-Jon, is the tallest temple in the country. Founded in 599 and further enlarged in 766, the entire complex was destroyed by the Japanese in 1592. It was rebuilt again in the mid-seventeenth century. The temple's approach road is lined with cherry and pine trees, and inside stands a huge gilt statue of Maitreya Buddha, 12 m (39 ft) tall, while outside is a superb six-tiered Paekche pagoda. In the nearby Nahan-jon, the second largest hall, sits a large Buddha surrounded by the figures of 500 disciples. Altogether there are ten cultural treasures preserved at this unusual temple.

From Chonju or the Kumsan Temple return to the Honam (Seoul-Sunchon) Expressway and proceed south to **Mt Naejang ("Inner Sanctum") National Park**, one of the best places in the country to enjoy autumn foliage. The main attraction here is the **Paegyang ("White Sheep") Temple**, a Zen temple established in 632. It has been destroyed four times since then and was rebuilt for a fifth time in 1917. A tourist hotel offers comfortable lodging for

ABOVE Almost shrouded by trees, the primitive dignity of the Unjin Miruk at Nonsan seems to owe more to the culture of the Easter Islands than China.

and tedious process.

At the foot of Mudong Mountain, which flanks the city, is a new resort with comfortable inns. At the Kwangju Museum are fascinating exhibits of relics recovered from a Chinese ship which sank near here 600 years ago, during China's Yuan dynasty. The displays include some excellent celadon vases and other porcelain ware in perfect condition.

Kwangju is a convenient launching point for tours of the southern coast of the country. For an abbreviated southern tour, proceed east along the expressway from Kwangju directly to Sunchon and head in the direction of Pusan.

CHUNGHAK-DONG

Accessible from the village of Hadong on the Pusan-Sunchon (Namhae) Expressway, Chunghak-dong is one of the handful of villages which have escaped the modernizing zeal of the Saemaul Movement, and here you may encounter Korean life as it was lived centuries ago. It is one Korea's most authentic pockets of classical Confucian culture and society.

Getting to it is rather difficult. From Hadong, about halfway between Kwangju and Pusan, buses depart three times in the morning and twice in the afternoon for the remote village of **Muke**, hidden in a valley on the eastern face of Mt Chiri. The two-hour drive by bus or car is rough and dusty the whole way. From Muke, another two hours of hard hiking will finally bring you to **Chunghak-dong**, nestled in a remote valley 860 m (2,822 ft) above sea level.

As in Hahoe, electricity and television have penetrated to this archaic village, but there is little other evidence of

the twentieth century. Unmarried men still wear their hair down their backs in long single braids, tying it up into traditional top-knots only after marriage. Education is still conducted in the classical Confucian manner by wizened teachers in horse-hair top hats, using Chinese characters in preference to *han'gul* and relying heavily on rote memorization. The clothing, the architecture and the atmosphere of Chunghak-dong are all straight out of a picture-book.

For visitors who wish to stay overnight there is a small *yogwan*, or they may impose on the hospitality of residents. In warm weather, some travelers hike in with their own camping gear, which considerably simplifies things.

CHINJU

Further along the expressway in the direction of Pusan is **Chinju**, a quintessentially Korean town seldom visited by foreigners, where a famous act of patriotic self-sacrifice took place.

Chinju Castle, recently renovated, was the site of two historic battles dur-

ABOVE Happy bather in Taejon, a provincial city in the throes of rapid modernization.

ing the Imjin War. During the first, the Japanese invaders were repulsed after fierce fighting, but a year later they attacked again, and this time the Korean forces were defeated and Chinju overrun. To celebrate their victory, Japanese officers held a great banquet at Choksongnu Pavilion in Chinju Castle. Among the women brought in to entertain them was the highly accomplished *kisaeng* Chu Non-gae, whose patron, a Korean officer, had been killed defending the town. During the party, Chu Non-gae plied an important Japanese general with wine, then lured him out for a stroll in the moonlight along a cliff overlooking the Nam River. At the edge of a steep precipice she suddenly threw her arms around him, and they toppled together to their deaths. Her patriotic sacrifice is marked every year with a ceremony at the shrine built in her honor above the rock from which she jumped.

MT CHIRI NATIONAL PARK

Northwest of Chinju is **Mt Chiri National Park.** Approaching it from the town of Kurye, you'll come across the **Hwaom Temple,** set in a steep valley which used to form the boundary between the ancient Shilla and Paekche kingdoms. Several national treasures are preserved here, including a four and a half meter (15 ft) stone lantern, the largest of its kind in Korea. The **Kahwangjon,** Awakening the Emperor Hall, a massive two-story structure with 49 m (160 ft) columns, is dedicated to the Chinese emperor who is said to have funded its construction during the eighth century.

Further into the hills is **Sanggye Temple,** established in 723 by a monk returning from China with the skull of the Zen patriarch Hui-Neng, which he had obtained through bribery. He erected a shrine in Mt Chiri to house his ill-gotten relic, and this developed into the Sanggye Temple.

NAMWON

Some 50 km (31 miles) north-east of Kwangju on the Kwangju-Taegu expressway is the old town of Namwon. For Koreans, Namwon is famous on account of the universally-known love story of Ch'unhyang and Myong-nyong, translated into English as *Fragrance* of Spring, which was located here and which has inspired countless Korean books, plays and movies. This is how the story goes:

Myong-nyong the son of a magistrate, fell in love with Ch'unhyang, the daughter of a *kisaeng*. Their romance blossomed and soon they married in secret, for there was no possibility that their parents would endorse such a match. Soon afterwards, Myong-nyong's father was transferred to a post in the capital, and the lovers were forced to separate. A corrupt and licentious governor was posted to Namwon, and he resolved to add the beautiful Ch'unhyang to his list of conquests. When she resisted him the enraged governor had her kidnaped, imprisoned and beaten. At this time, however, Myong-nyong was appointed Royal Inspector for Cholla Province, and when he heard what had happened to his beloved he rushed to her rescue and severely punished the governor. Bride and groom returned to Seoul, where they lived happily ever after. Ch'unhyang's fidelity is celebrated annually on the eighth day of the fourth lunar month (around mid-March) at a shrine in Namwon erected in her honor.

Chiri itself is a range of stark granite peaks and thickly wooded valleys. Due to the great variety of flowering fruit trees and deciduous foliage, the park is especially enchanting in spring and autumn. It is said that when tea was introduced into Korea from China during the Shilla era, it was first cultivated on

the sunny slopes of this mountain.

SONGGWANG TEMPLE

From Mt Chiri Park return to Kurye and proceed due south about 40 km (25 miles) to Sunchon. From there a regular bus runs to **Songgwang Temple**, one of the three largest in the country and the center of the Son (Zen) sect. It's a delightful ride the whole way. If you are visiting the temple from Pusan, the express bus to Sunchon takes four hours. If you are coming from Kwangju, the bus trip takes only an hour.

Songgwang Temple was originally established as a hermitage during the Shilla era, but was expanded into a full-scale temple during the twelfth century by the great Son master Pojo and his disciples. It has many exquisite examples of traditional Korean temple architecture from different periods; the two covered, arched bridges which cross the small stream at the temple's entrance, for example, architectural features seldom seen elsewhere.

Today Songgwang Temple has become famous for its small but permanent contingent of resident foreign monks and nuns. When they enter the order, the aspiring bonzes must first spend three to six months doing kitchen duty and maintenance work. They then embark on a strict regimen of meditation, supplemented by regular stints of farm work. Most of the foreigners speak little or no Korean, yet they seem to get on harmoniously with their Korean dharma brethren. Visitors can stay overnight in the temple, which also provides delicious Buddhist vegetarian meals.

ISLAND HOPPING

The ferry terminus for excursions to islands off Korea's southwestern coast is **Mokp'o**, a rather dreary old shipping town with little of interest for the visitor, though the trails up Mt Yudal, the rocky, two-peaked mountain which straddles the town, may be considered an attraction of sorts.

Mokp'o is a convenient launching-pad for island-hoppers. The longest excursion possible is the eight-hour trip west to **Hongdo, "Red Island,"** renowned for its fiery groves of blossoming camellia and its rock formations. There is no accommodation here, but you will find food and lodging on nearby Huk Island, from where boats may be hired to go to Hongdo.

More convenient is Chindo, an island

only a few hours' south of Mokp'o by ferry. **Chindo** is known for its characteristic breed of dog, and as a center of shamanism.

There are many other islands in the area offering ample opportunities for swimming, fishing and boating, but the region is far less oriented to tourism than other parts of the country. It is thus well suited to the intrepid - though, like the rest of the country, the local buses are frequent and the cheap inns numerous.

Country life: OPPOSITE, country gent takes a stroll in the midday sun; ABOVE on some farms, oxen continue to earn their keep alongside more modern contraptions.

169

Travelers'
Tips

ARRIVING AND DEPARTING

Korea may be entered from abroad through three international airports: Kimp'o, near Seoul; Kimhae, near Pusan; and Cheju, near Cheju City. All three are modern and well-equipped.

At present 15 airlines provide regular jet service to and from Korea, with over 200 scheduled flights weekly. Korean Air (KE), United Air Lines (UA) and Northwest Orient (NW) connect Seoul with Los Angeles, New York and Honolulu. The same carriers plus Japan Air Lines (JL) serve Tokyo, while Korean Air and Cathay Pacific (CX) are among the airlines that fly from Seoul to Hong Kong, Taipei, Kuala Lumpur and Bangkok. Singapore Airlines (SQ), Thai International (TG), China Airlines (CI) and Malaysia Airlines (MH) are among the other flag-carriers that link Seoul with Taipei and points beyond in South-east Asia. Paris, Zurich, Frankfurt and Amsterdam are the European capitals served by at least one carrier flying out of Seoul.

Tokyo and Taipei are the two nearest capital cities to Seoul, both a little over two hours' flying-time distant. A stop in Seoul may be included in round-the-world or North-east Asian tickets at no extra charge.

Below is a list of airline offices in Seoul, both on-line and off-line carriers. The prefix for Seoul when dialing from elsewhere is 02.

Passenger Airlines Serving Korea:
Air France, Room 218, Chosun Hotel, 87, Sogong-dong. Tel: 753- 2574.
Cathay Pacific Airways, Room 701, Kolon Building, 45 Mugyo-dong. Tel: 779-0321/6.
China Airlines, Room 211, Chosun Hotel, 87 Sogong-dong. Tel: 755-1523/5.

Japan Air Lines, Room 101, Paiknam Building, 188-3, 1-ga, Ulchiro. Tel: 757-1711.
KLM Royal Dutch Airlines, Room 110, Chosun Hotel, 87 Sogong-dong. Tel: 753-1093.
Korean Air, KAL Building, 118, 2-ga, Namdaemunno. Tel: 771-66.
Kuwait Airways, Room 236, Chosun Hotel, 87 Sogong-dong. Tel: 753-0041/3.
Lufthansa German Airlines, Room 105, Chosun Hotel, 87 Sogong- dong. Tel: 777-9655/6.
Malaysian Airline System, 14th floor, Dongbang Life Insurance Main Building, 150, 2-ga, T'aep'yongno. Tel: 777-7761/2.
Northwest Orient Airlines, Room 201, Chosun Hotel, 87 Sogong- dong. Tel: 753-6106/9.
United Airways, Room 503, New Korea Building, 19-11, 1-ga, Ulchiro. Tel: 777-2993/7.
Saudi Arabian Airlines, 13th floor, Daeyeonkak Building, 25-5, 1-ga, Ch'ungmuro. Tel: 755-5621/2.
Singapore Airlines, Room 202, Chosun Hotel, 87 Sogong-dong. Tel: 755-1226/8.
Thai Airways International Ltd, Room 208, Chosun Hotel, 87 Sogong-dong. Tel: 779-2621/5.

Airlines With Offices in Seoul But No Direct Flights:
Air India, Room 225, Chosun Hotel, 87 Sogong-dong. Tel: 778-0064.
Alitalia Airlines, Room 111, Chosun Hotel, 87 Sogong-dong. Tel: 779-1676/8.
American Airlines Inc., Room 103, Chosun Hotel, 87 Sogong-dong. Tel: 778-3351/3.
British Airways, Room 801, Dongmin Building, 95 Mugyo-dong. Tel: 777-6871/5.
British Caledonian Airways, Room 238, Chosun Hotel, 87 Sogong-dong. Tel: 777-8131/3.

Canadian Pacific Airlines, Room 105, Chosun Hotel, 87 Sogong-dong. Tel: 753-8271.

Continental Airlines, Room 707, New Korea Building, 192-11, 1-ga, Ulchiro. Tel: 778-0394/5.

Delta Airlines, Room 234, Chosun Hotel, 87 Sogong-dong. Tel: 753-3202.

Eastern Airlines, Room 108, Chosun Hotel, 87 Sogong-dong. Tel: 777-9786/8.

Egypt Air, Seojin Building, 149-1 P'yong-dong. Tel: 725-1401/5.

El Al Israel Airlines, Room 1302, Samkoo Building, 70 Sogong-dong. Tel: 755-1345.

Gulf Air, Room 111, Chosun Hotel, 87 Sogong-dong. Tel: 779-1676/8.

Philippine Airlines, Seojin Building, 149-1, P'yong-dong. Tel: 725-1401/3.

Qantas Airways Ltd., Room 801, Dongmin Building, 95 Mugyo-dong. Tel: 777-6875.

Republic Airlines, Room 707, New Korea Building, 192-11, 1-ga, Ulchiro. Tel: 755-8945.

Sabena Airlines, Room 707, New Korea Building, 192-11, 1-ga, Ulchiro. Tel: 778-0394.

Scandinavian Airlines System, Room 220, Chosun Hotel, 87 Sogong-dong. Tel: 752-5123/4.

Swiss Air Transport Co. Ltd., Room 205, Chosun Hotel, 87 Sogong-dong. Tel: 777-4864/5.

Varig Brazilian Airlines, Room 505, New Korea Building, 192-11, 1-ga, Ulchiro. Tel: 755-8945.

Western Airlines, Room 707, New Korea Building, 192-11, 1-ga, Ulchiro. Tel: 755-8945.

Airport Tax

All passengers leaving Korea by air are required to pay an airport tax of ₩5,000.

Baggage Allowance

On all flights other than those from the United States and US territories, the baggage allowance is 30 kg (66 lb) for first-class adult passengers and 20 kg (44 lb) for economy-class adults. On all flights from the United States and US territories, passengers are allowed to take two bags, each weighing not more than 35 kg (77 lb).

Transport from Airport to Town

Kimp'o – Downtown Seoul:
Whichever way you go it will take about 35 minutes. Exception: the local city bus, which takes about 50 (fare: ₩130), but is available only at domestic airport terminals. Airport bus 601 (₩500), City express bus 63 or 68 (₩350) and local city bus 41 all go to City Hall, near the principal hotels. A taxi will take you there for about ₩2,700, a call taxi for roughly twice that. In fact, nearly all the taxis operating out of Kimp'o are call taxis.

Kimhae to Downtown Pusan:
1 hour by airport bus (₩320), 50 minutes by taxi.

Cheju Airport to downtown Cheju: Ten minutes by taxi or hotel bus, 20 minutes, by airport bus (₩200).

DOMESTIC AIR SERVICE

All air services within Korea are handled by Korean Air, which schedules over 100 flights a week between Seoul and Pusan (50 minutes), Cheju (55 minutes), Taegu (50 minutes) and other popular destinations. For information, either visit the head office in Seoul, KAL Building, 118, 2-ga, Namdaemunno, Chung-gu or call (02) 771-66. To make KAL bookings around the country, call the following numbers:

Seoul: (02) 756-2000;
Pusan: (051) 44-0131;
Cheju: (0641) 2-6111;
Kwangju: (062) 232-0551/3;
Taegu: (053) 423-4231;
Yosu: (0662) 62-8123/4; Sokch'o: (0392) 2-2400;
Chinju: (0591) 53-3906/7;
Ulsan: (0522) 75-8221.
Because of the peninsula's political

divide, strict security measures are enforced on all Korean domestic flights. For example, cameras, radios and even liquor (an "inflammable liquid") may not be brought into the cabin but must be placed in special containers in the cargo hold and collected at one's destination.

TRAINS

Korea's rail service is efficient and comfortable, and is particularly useful for traveling between major cities. Journeys to smaller towns are usually quicker by bus. Five types of train are operated:

Wanhaeng: "locals" which stop at every station;

Potong kuphaeng: regular express trains with numerous stops; some are night trains with sleeping berths;

Tukkup: limited express trains, some with dining cars; seats may be reserved;

Udung: trains with air-conditioned or heated cars;

Saemaul: super-express trains with air-conditioning/heating and dining cars.

Saemaul trains are the fastest, most comfortable and most expensive, and connect Seoul with the other major cities, stopping a few times in between. Sample times:

Seoul-Pusan, 4 hours and 40 minutes;

Seoul-Mokp'o, 5 hours and 30 minutes;

Seoul-Kyongju, 4 hours and 40 minutes.

Seats on *Saemaul* trains may be reserved up to ten days in advance through local travel agencies. It is wise to book ahead in summer, when many Koreans are on the move. The stations of major cities have special counters to help visitors with language problems. The numbers are as follows:

Seoul: (02) 392-7788, ext: 2178;

Taejon: (042) 253-7451;

Taegu: (053) 92-0460;

Pusan: (051) 463-5782;

Kyongju: (0561) 2-7788;

Yongju: (0572) 2-1330.

The main office of Korean National Railroads is at 168, 2-ga, Pongnae-dong, Chung-gu, Seoul. Tel: (02) 392-0078.

BUSES

Highway express buses operated by ten different companies connect all major cities and towns via the nation's excellent and under-used highways. There are three types of buses: *kosok*, fast super-express; *chikhaeng*, first-class local service; and *wanhaeng*, regular local buses with frequent stops.

Express buses are fast and comfortable, but some visitors avoid them due to their reputation for getting involved in nasty accidents. The buses are so frequent and convenient, however, that only the super-prudent would abide by this rule. It is possible to book bus tickets ahead, but those who don't and just turn up at the terminus will rarely have to wait more than half an hour before the next bus leaves.

All express buses from Seoul depart from **Kangnam Kosok Express Bus Terminal** on the south side of the Han River in Banpo-dong. Subway line no.3 stops there: the station is **Express Bus Terminal** (in English).

The phone numbers of Seoul's ten express bus companies are as follows:

Chonil: 598-3166;

Chungang: 591-0128;

Hanil: 598-2101;

Hanjin: 598-2725;

Kolon: 598-2008;

Kwangju: 598-2071;

Samhwa: 598-2781;

Songnisan: 598-3358;

Tongbu: 599-1865;

Tongyang: 598-3111.

Buses from Seoul to less distant destinations leave from the following major bus terminals:

Tongbu Bus Terminal. Tel: 792-3791; in Majang-dong. Buses to Ch'unch'on,

Mt Sorak, Sokch'o, Yangyang, Yong-mun Temple, Kangnung, Yoju, Ch'ung-ju, Kwang-ju, Andong.

Nambu Bus Terminal, tel: 966-6762; on the main road in south Yongsan. Buses to Kanghwa Island, Kosam, Tae-chon Beach, Puyo, Kongju, Chonju, Mt Songni, Ch'ongju, Taechon.

Shinchon Bus Terminal, tel: 34-0611; at Shinch'on Rotary. Buses to Kanghwa Island (one-and-a-quarter hours).

Miari Bus Terminal, tel: 980-7638; in the north of the city. Buses direct to Mt Soyo, handy for trekkers and climbers.

Chonho-dong Bus Terminal, tel: 48-2159; southeast of Seoul. Buses to Southern Han Mountain Fortress (Nam-hansansong) and Kwangju.

Yok Chon Bus Terminal, across the street from Seoul Station. Buses to Inch'on, (tel: 755-2221) and to Pyongtaek, (tel: 779-0101).

Seoul Sobu Bus Terminal, tel: 388-5103. In Pulgwang-dong; buses to Haenju, Sansong, Uichongbu.

TAXIS AND RENTED CARS

Taxis are the simplest way of getting around in Korean cities, and visitors arriving from the West will regard them as a bargain. The current fare, which has not changed for some time, is ₩600 for the first two kilometers and ₩50 for each additional 400 meters. From midnight to 4 am a 20 per cent surcharge is added, and in Seoul fares pay ₩50 for every 96 seconds in addition to the basic fare when the cab runs at less than 15 kph. Tipping is unnecessary unless the driver helps with luggage.

The difficult thing about taxis in Seoul (and to a lesser extent in Pusan) is finding one that is willing to take you. Always know where you want to go and shout it through the window of the cruising cab. The driver will then stop or not, depending on whether it seems to make sense to him to take you. If desperate and not short of money, take a cab from one of the major hotels, where more expensive call taxis and tourist taxis are often available. There are many roofed-over pickup points around the city. In a regular taxi you may well be expected to share the ride with two or more other passengers - though you will normally have to pay the full fare. But apart from this minor fiddle Korea's taxi-drivers are models of probity, and their meters are kept in good working order.

Call taxis are larger than the regular and are colored gold. The fare is ₩1,000 for the first two kilometers and ₩100 for each additional 400 meters. They may be hailed on the street or at taxi-stops like regular cabs.

Tourist taxis are even larger and more expensive and are usually found at the big hotels. Fares begin at ₩2,000. They can also be hired for fixed periods: ₩8,000 an hour, ₩35,000 for 4 hours, ₩65,000 a day (10 hours). Tel: (02) 333-1238 for more information.

The most comfortable as well as

PREVIOUS PAGES: Country women on a trip pose for a memorial photo in the garden of Seoul's Kyongbok Palace. ABOVE Seoul's central train station, another relic of the Japanese occupation.

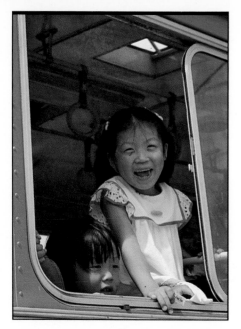

Airport and in the lobbies of the Chosun and Lotte hotels. **Cheju Rent Car** in Cheju has 45 cars; check at Cheju Airport. Sample prices:

Pony: ₩26,000 for 12 hours, ₩35,000 for 24 hours.

Rekord Prince: ₩33,000 for 12 hours, ₩47,000 for 24 hours.

Drivers must be over 21 and have a valid passport and international license.

Chauffeur-driven cars: fees include driver, fuel, insurance charge and 10% Value Added Tax. Turnpike and parking fees not included. Sample prices:

Pony: ₩8,200 an hour / 21 km; ₩49,000 a day (6-10 hours / 125 km);

Rekord Prince: ₩11,000 an hour, ₩66,000 a day.

costly way to see Korea is by private car, either self- or chauffeur-driven. Five excellent expressways slice through and across the peninsula:

Kyongbu (Seoul-Pusan),
Honam (Taechon-Kwangju),
Yongdong (Suwon-Kangnung),
Namhae (Kwangju-Sunchon-Masan-Pusan) and
'88 Olympic Expressway (Kwangju-Taegu).

These and the ancillary county roads pass through Korea's most scenic mountains, valleys and farm-lands, and they are a pleasure to drive on. The inflated price of gasoline may hurt your pocket but it keeps the roads pleasantly empty.

As yet, Korea's car rental system remains underdeveloped, and Seoul and Cheju are the only places where cars may be rented. **Hertz Korean Rent-a-Car** in Seoul has 320 cars available (tel: (02) 585-0801/5, (02) 798-0801/3, (02) 724-7465), and offices at Kimp'o

SEOUL'S SUBWAY

Lines 3 and 4 have recently been added to the system, bringing its length to 116.5 kilometers (72 miles) and making it the world's seventh longest subway. Seoul's subway is cheap, fast, clean, safe, and less crowded than Tokyo's (a little). No smoking in the trains, which turn up roughly every five minutes. There are only two fares, ₩200 and ₩300 according to zone.

FERRIES

There are two ways of entering Korea by sea from Japan. The most useful is the **Pukwan Ferry** which plies between Shimonoseki and Pusan every day except Saturdays. Departure time at both ends is 5 pm. The crossing takes seven hours, but disembarking is delayed until morning to allow passengers a full night's rest. Single fares range from US$40 (second class) to US$70 (special first class). Further information: in Seoul, (02) 752-9716, (02) 753-1339; in Pusan, (051) 463-3165/8; in Shimonoseki, (0832) 66-8211; in Tokyo, (03) 567-0974; in Osaka, (06) 345-2245.

ABOVE Cheerful passengers aboard a bus in Seoul: one of the easiest ways to see the city - if you can read Han'gul.

The **Kukche Ferry** links Japan's second city, Osaka, with Pusan. The ferry sails twice a week, leaving Osaka at 2 pm on Tuesday and Friday and departing Pusan on Sunday and Wednesday at 6 pm. The crossing takes 21 hours and fares range from $71 to $150. For further details contact (02) 784-3333 in Seoul, (051) 463-7000 in Pusan and (06) 266-1111 in Osaka.

Numerous domestic ferries sail between Korea's coastal towns and offshore islands. The following are the most useful and important:

Pusan-Cheju Car Ferry: Departure (from both ports): 7:30 pm, daily except Sundays. Length of crossing: eleven-and-a-half hours. Fares range from ₩10,780 (third class) to ₩78,040 (special class); price for vehicles ranges from ₩48,400 to ₩21,000. Advance ticket sales:

    Seoul: (02) 730-7316;
    Pusan: (051) 463-0605;
    Cheju: (0641) 2-0291;
    Mokp'o: (0631) 2-9391.

Mokp'o-Cheju Car Ferry: Mokp'o

departure 4 pm daily except Sundays; Cheju departure, 7 am daily except Mondays. Length of crossing: five-and-a-half hours. Fares range from ₩7,340 (third class) to ₩57,800 (special class); price for vehicles ranges from ₩41,600 to ₩104,000. Advance ticket sales: as above.

P'ohang-Ullung Island: One round trip a day during summer (May-August). P'ohang departure: 10 pm, Ullung departure 9:30 am. Year-round daily service: departs P'ohang, Ullung 10 am. Length of crossing: 7 hours. Fares range from ₩11,770 (second class) to ₩17,650 (first-class berth). Advance sales:

    Seoul: (02) 598-2101;
    P'ohang: (0562) 2-0711;
    Ullung: 2602.

Pusan-Ch'ungmu-Yosu Hydrofoil: The hydrofoil "Angel" skims the length of the Hallyo Waterway, traveling six

---

ABOVE Theoretically more convenient than buses, Seoul's taxis can be very troublesome, as some of the faces in this line eloquently suggest.

times a day from Pusan to Ch'ungmu (with stops in Songp'o) and three times daily between Ch'ungmu and Yosu (with stops in Samch'onp'o and Namhae). Length of trip: Pusan-Ch'ungmu: one-and-a-half hours; Ch'ungmu-Yosu: 1 hour and 50 minutes. Sample fares: Pusan-Ch'ungmu, ₩6,250; Pusan-Yosu: ₩12,300. For reservations call:

Seoul (02) 734-5636;
Pusan: (051) 44-3851;
Ch'ungmu: (0557) 2-2091;
Yosu: (0662) 63-2824.

like within the period indicated, as long as they do not work:

Austria: 90 days;
Bangladesh: 90 days;
Belgium: 60 days;
Chile: 90 days;
Colombia: 90 days;
Costa Rica: 90 days;
Denmark: 60 days;
Dominican Rep.: 90 days;
Finland: 60 days;
France: 30 days;
West Germany: 60 days;
Greece: 3 months days;

ENTRY FORMALITIES

Foreigners wishing to enter Korea must have a valid passport or entry permit. Those with confirmed outbound tickets may stay for up to 15 days without a visa. Visitors from the following countries are allowed to stay as long as they

Iceland: 60 days;
Italy: 60 days;
Lesotho: 60 days;
Liberia: 90 days;
Luxemburg: 60 days;
Mexico: 3 months;
Malaysia: 3 months;
Netherlands: 60 days;
Norway: 60 days;
Peru: 90 days;
Portugal: 60 days;
Singapore: 90 days;
Spain: 60 days;
Surinam: 60 days;

ABOVE Building the subway cost Seoul a fortune it does not possess, but it has made life considerably easier for residents.

Sweden: 60 days;
Switzerland: 3 months;
Thailand: 90 days;
Tunisia: 30 days;
Turkey: 60 days;
United Kingdom: 60 days.

Visitors from other countries who plan to stay longer than 15 days can obtain a visa from a Korean Embassy or Consulate before coming to the country. Visas are of two types: up to 90 days, for tourists; and longer than 90 days, for which an entry permit must be obtained from the Ministry of Justice. All who stay longer than 90 days must also apply for a residence certificate at the local District Immigration Ofice. To extend a visa, visit the District Immigration Office at least one day before the visa expires.

These are the addresses and phone numbers of the principle immigration offices:

Immigration Bureau, Ministry of Justice, 2nd Unified Government Building, 1, Chungang-ri, Kwach'on-myon, Shihung-gun, Kyonggi-do. Tel: (02) 503-7096.

Seoul Immigration Office: 39-1, Sosomun-dong, Chung-gu, Seoul. Tel: (02) 776-8984/7.

Kimp'o Immigration Office: Kimp'o International Airport, Seoul. Tel: (02) 662-7611/5.

Pusan Immigration Office, 17-27, 4-ga, Chungang-dong, Chung-gu, Pusan, Tel: (051) 463-7161/5.

Kimhae Immigration Office, Kimhae International Airport, Kyongsangnam-do, Tel: (051) 98-1871/3.

Cheju Immigration Office, 740-3, Konip-dong, Cheju, Cheju Island. Tel: (0641) 2-3494/5.

CUSTOMS

You can bring the following items into Korea without paying duty: two bottles of spirits (up to 760 cc each), 400 cigarettes, 50 cigars, 250 g pipe tobacco, 100 g snuff or other tobacco, or any combination within the limit of 500 g in total. If you bring in books, other printed matter, films, records or anything else that the authorities deem subversive, you're likely to lose them.

EXPORT

There are strict limits on the export of items more than 50 years old, specimens of wildlife (live or stuffed), and ginseng. Get your permit for the export of an tiques from the **Cultural Property**

Preservation Bureau, near Kyongbokkung Palace, Seoul, tel: (02) 725-3053. For five or fewer pieces, permits may also be obtained from the bureau's Kimp'o Airport branch office, tel: (02) 662-0106.

QUARANTINE

Visitors entering from cholera-affected regions should carry a vaccination certificate. Animals and animal products, plants and plant products must all be declared on arrival. Dogs and cats must be accompanied by a veterinarian health certificate issued at point of origin and a rabies vaccination certificate. They are subject to a quarantine period of

ABOVE The cheapest way to enter Korea from abroad is on the Pusan-Shimonoseki ferry from Japan. It sails every day except Saturday, and completes the crossing in seven hours.

10 days.

CLIMATE AND CLOTHING

Korea gets it all ways: it's bitter in winter and sticky in summer. In between it has some of the world's nicest weather, and the wheeling of its four distinct seasons is a pleasure in its own right.

Spring: The spring thaw begins in April and the season lasts until mid-June. Average temperatures range between 10-16°C (50-60°F) in Seoul. Spring weather is warm but changeable, with not infrequent showers. Take lightweight clothes for this season, plus a few lightweight sweaters and jackets for cool evenings and chilly mountain air.

Summer: Summer proper is preceded by a month-long rainy season, then from mid-July to mid-September the weather is hot and humid with occasional thunder showers. Temperatures range from 18-24°C (65-75°F) in the north to 24-30°C (75-85°F) in the south. Appropriate summer clothing would include light cotton sports shirts, loose-fitting pants, swimsuits, and some form of light rain gear.

Autumn: The best season to travel through Korea, fall lasts from mid-September to mid-November, as Siberian northerlies re-enact their yearly battle with Pacific southerlies. Average temperatures range between 12-18°C (55-65°F) and the weather is distinguished by long periods of brilliantly clear, dry weather. Lightweight clothes, with sweaters and jackets for evening and mountains, will see you through.

Winter: Lasts from mid-November to March and ranges from cold to bitter. In January and February temperatures are down between -12° to 2°C (10-35°F). Appropriate clothing would include warm woolen pants, heavy shirts, heavy sweaters and jackets, a winter overcoat, and long underwear if you intend to visit any national parks.

CURRENCY

The unit of Korean currency is won (₩). Coin denominations are ₩1, ₩5, ₩10, ₩50, ₩100. Banknotes come in ₩500, ₩1,000, ₩5,000 and ₩10,000 denominations.

The exchange rate fluctuates, but at the time of going to press US$1 = ₩780. Foreign currencies can be converted at banks, hotels and other authorized money-changers around the country. Any amount larger than $5,000 must be declared when entering the country. Unused won may be re-converted into foreign currencies up to a limit of $1,000. You can only take out as much foreign currency as you declared on arrival.

Major credit cards such as American Express, Visa, MasterCharge and Diner's Club are accepted at most large hotels, department stores and restaurants in the big cities.

COMMUNICATIONS

MAIL

Seoul's central post office is located on Ch'ungmu Road, a block east of Shinsegye Department Store, just across from the Chinese Embassy. There are convenient branch offices near the intersection of T'aep'yong and Chong Streets, and on Yulkok Street near the Anguk Immigration Office. Stamps are available in most hotels.

Regular stamped letters and postcards may be dropped into any mailbox, but all overseas parcels must be mailed and picked up at the International Post Office across from Yonsei

University in Yonhi-dong. All incoming and outgoing mail in Korea is subject to government inspection. Delivery time to and from Europe and America is 9-14 days, while local mail takes 2-3. Post office hours are 9 am to 5 pm Monday through Friday and 9 am to 1 pm on Saturday.

TELEPHONES

Local calls may be dialed from the red and green public phones found in hotels, public buildings and booths around the country. Two ten-won coins must be inserted after lifting the receiver and before dialing; calls are automatically terminated after three minutes.

Long distance calls within Korea may be made from the large yellow pay phones in hotels, post offices and on the street. Both ten-won and hundred-won coins may be used, and when you hear bleeps it is time to insert more money. Unused coins are automatically returned when you hang up.

Area codes within Korea are as follows:

Seoul 02
Pusan 051
Taegu 053
Inch'on and Puchon 032
Kanghwa 0349
Kimp'o 034
Tongduch'on 0351
Munsan 0348
Songnam 0342
Suwon 0331
Anyang 0343
Yoju 0337
Osan 0339
Yong-in 0335
Uijongbu 0351
Ich'on 0336
Kangnung 0391
Tonghae 0394
Sokch'o 0392
Wonju 0371
Ch'olwon 0353
Ch'unch'on 0361
Samch'ok 039
Ch'ongju 0431
Ch'ungju 0441
Kongju 0416
Taejon 042
Puyo 0463
Onyang 0418
Ch'onan 0417
Kunsan 0654
Namwon 0671
Iri 0653
Chonju 0652
Kwangju 062
Mokp'o 0631
Yosu 0662
Kyongju 0561
Andong 0571
P'ohang 0562
Masan and Ch'angwon 0551
Ulsan 0522
Chinju 0591
Chinhae 0553
Ch'ungmu 0557
Sogwip'o 0642
Cheju 0641

International calls: You can place international calls through the operators at major hotels, or at the International Telecommunications Exchange, on Sejong Road, near the Sejong Cultural Center. Seventy-five countries may be dialed from phones connected to the International Subscriber Dialing (ISD) system by first dialing the international access code (001) then the country and area codes and the individual number. For further details dial 1030. For operator-assisted calls, dial 1035 or 1037 in Seoul and 117 elsewhere.

Telegrams: You may write out telegrams at the International Telecommunications Building on Sejong Road or dictate them over the phone by dialing 115. The former method is surer. "Urgent" telegrams take 6 hours, "Ordinary," 12 hours, and "Letter Telegrams," 24 hours. The International Telecommunications Building is open from 9 am to 5 pm

Monday to Friday and 9 am to 1 pm on Saturday.

RADIO AND TELEVISION

Twiddle the knobs of your hotel radio and you'll find a rich assortment of soap operas, traditional and Western music and unfathomable news and discussion programs. Four major radio stations broadcast nationwide, and in addition the **American Forces Korea Network** broadcasts news and music exclusively in English 24 hours a day, with international news reports every hour on the hour.

Likewise the two major Korean TV stations, whose soaps and commercials give wonderful insights into the state of contemporary Korean culture, are usefully augmented by **AFKN-TV** which broadcasts popular American comedy shows, movies and news programs.

NEWSPAPERS, PERIODICALS AND OTHER PUBLICATIONS

Six nationally distributed newspapers are currently published in Korea, in-cluding one in Chinese and two in English. They appear daily except for Mondays and national holidays. The two English language papers are the *Korea Herald* and the *Korea Times*. Neither is a giant of the newspaper world, and most of their stories are drawn from the wire services. The president is usually on the front page, patting small heads, while riots and other uncongenial domestic matters are relegated to the back. Both papers are available in hotels, kiosks and news stands throughout the country. Other English-language papers available in Korea are the *Asian Wall Street Journal,* the *International Herald Tribune* and the Pacific edition of *Stars and Stripes,* the American military paper.

English language periodicals published in Korea include *Korea Journal* (published by UNESCO), and the weekly *Korea News Review,* a digest of the *Korea Herald. Korea Quarterly* is an English language magazine of Korean culture.

ABOVE Buddha's Birthday celebration at Chogye-sa Temple, Seoul's principal Buddhist temple.

Foreign periodicals available in Korea include *Time, Newsweek* and the *Far East Economic Review.* All foreign publications brought into Korea are subject to government censorship, though this has been gradually relaxed in the past few years.

The best place in Seoul to find English language books, whether on Korean or other subjects, is the bookstore in the basement of the Kyobo Building, opposite Sejong Cultural Center. English language books on Korean subjects are found in the Government Publications section.

ACCOMMODATION

For visitors with a modicum of flexibility, accommodation is not a serious problem in Korea. Hotels of international quality are found only in the major cities and resorts, but clean and decent accommodation of a more modest order is found everywhere. The lists of hotels, inns and hostels which follow descriptions of major destinations in **The Broad Highway** will be useful for those who care to book in advance and like to see every step of the way ahead of them. Others may prefer to memorize the *han'gul* characters for the different species of inn and try their luck on arrival.

YOGWAN

International hotels need no explanation, but the Korean varieties of ordinary hotel, inn and hostel have certain peculiarities.

Essentially, ordinary hotels and inns *(yogwan,* written 여관 in *han'gul)* are distinguished only by the facilities they provide and the rates they charge. In an ordinary hotel, as defined by the authorities, each room has its own bathroom with toilet and running h and c; the room is air-conditioned and furnished Western-style. The *yogwan* is an inn where over one-third of the rooms are equipped with their own bathrooms. You may be provided with a regular Western bed or with a Korean *yo* (mattress or futon), *ibul* (quilt) and *pyogae* (pillow). There may or may not be some Western furniture; either way the floor will probably be heated by *ondol* (except in summer), and air-conditioning will be in the form of an electric fan. The guest will normally be expected to take his meals in the town, and to pay for the room when checking in. A night at a *yogwan* will cost around ₩10,900; at an ordinary hotel, between ₩12,700 (for a smaller or *Ul* hotel) and ₩15,000 (for larger so-called *Kap* hotels).

What the *yogwan* will not normally provide is the ambience of old Korea: the large majority are bald concrete boxes, just like the hotels. The Japanese word *ryokan* and the Korean *yogwan* are written with the same Chinese characters (they mean "travel building"), but equivalents of Japan's elegant traditional *ryokan* are sadly rare; possibly the best in the country is the Un Dang Yogwan described in the **Seoul** section of **The Broad Highway,** above.

YOINSOOK

The one category of accommodation which retains much of the atmosphere of the old days is so humble that the Korea National Tourism Corporation does not even care for foreigners to know about it, yet for seekers of the curious and characteristic as well as travelers on tight budgets, the *yoinsook* demands to be tried.

The *yoinsook* (여인숙 in *han'gul)* is the category of inn below the *yogwan,* and they are found in great quantity in every town and city, usually close to train and bus stations. The building may be a low, traditional one, with a heavy tile roof, and the rooms may open off a courtyard. Facilities are basic: ashtray, towel, tea, bedding which the guest spreads out himself. The communal bathroom is likely to have cold water only and the lavatory may lack plumbing, but in general the standards of cleanliness are decent. Some have improbably archaic views of forgotten corners of the city from their windows; some have caged peacocks at the front gate or guests who sing all night. It's a matter of pot luck. Room rates may be as low as ₩4,000 or as high as ₩8,000 a night, depending on the facilities provided. As with all hotels and inns in the country, rates are fixed by the government and you get as much or as little as you pay for.

Youth hostels are another possibility. At present there are only 20 in the whole country, all located at popular resorts such as Mt Sorak and Kyongju. Besides the familiar dormitory accommodation, most provide double rooms as well. Principal ones are listed in **The Broad Highway** under particular destinations. For information about others, contact the **Korea Youth Hostel Association,** 27-1, Sup'yo-dong, Chung-gu, Seoul. Tel: (02) 66- 2896.

TOURIST INFORMATION

Korea attracted 1,093,000 foreign visitors in 1981 and nearly 1,300,000 in 1984, and the number is bound to continue rising during the coming years. Evidence of how seriously the government takes this important source of foreign exchange is seen in the efforts made to enable visitors to enjoy themselves. The Korea National Tourism Corporation (KNTC) has a big headquarters building in Seoul with an excellent new information center in the basement. There are several other information centers and counters in Seoul and other

OPPOSITE Acrobatics at the annual spring festival in Namwon, honoring Korea's favorite literary heroine, Ch'unhyang.

cities, and one complaint center. Details are provided below. Besides helping with maps, pamphlets and hotel directories, they also have specialized literature to advise people planning to hold conventions in the country. KNTC is not a travel agent, however. For practical help with reservations and tickets, contact one of the travel agents further down.

KNTC Head Office: KNTC Building, 10, Ta-dong, Chung-gu, Seoul. Tel: (02) 757-6030.
Kimp'o Airport Information Center: 1st floor, Airport Terminal Building, Kimp'o International Airport, Seoul. Tel: (02) 662- 2182/3.
Kimhae Airport Information Center: 218 Taejo 2-dong, Puk-gu, Pusan. Tel: (051) 98-1100.
Cheju Airport Information Center: 2096 Yongdam-dong, 3-do, Cheju. Tel: (0641) 7-0528.
Seoul Tourist Information Center: The center (directly behind City Hall. Tel: (02) 731 6337) is open 9 am to 6 pm Monday to Friday, 9 am to 1 pm Saturday. The center also has the following information counters:
Kimp'o International Airport Terminal, tel: 662-9248.
Seoul Railway Station, tel: 779-3643.
Seoul Express Bus Terminal, tel: 598-4152.
Chongno, tel: 734-0023.
Kwanghwamun, tel: 734-0027.
Myong-dong, tel: 779-3645.
Namdaemun, tel: 779-3644.
Tongdaemun, tel: 272-0348.

If something seems badly wrong, contact **KNTC Tourist Complaint Center** in Seoul, tel: 725-0101. If you want to make a complaint when you are outside Seoul, dial the area code followed by 0101 and you will be put through to the tourist administration section of the local government. Exceptions: **Kyongju,** tel: (0561) 2-8000; **Sokch'o,** tel: (0392) 2-3171/7; **Kyongsangnam-do Prov-**

ince, tel: (0451) 22-1792.

Goodwill Guides Campaign

The run-up to the Olympics will surely show an increase in the number of volunteer "goodwill guides" roaming the streets and helping foreign visitors who are in trouble. They wear badges with smiling faces superimposed on the national yin-yang emblem.

TRAVEL AGENTS

These are the Seoul addresses and phone numbers of some of the major ones:

Aju Tourist Service Co. Ltd., 21-1, Sosomun-dong, Chung-gu. Tel: (03) 753-5051/4.

Chowon Tourist Co. Ltd., 1st and 11th floor, Konpyong Building, 5-1, Konpying-dong, Chongno-gu. Tel: 744-5544/6.

Dong Yang Express Travel Service Inc., 84-18, 5-ga, Namdaemunno, Chung-gu. Tel: 753-0011/4.

Far East Tours Ltd, 4 Floor Namyong Building, 809-16 Yoksam-dong, Kangnam-gu. Tel: 561-0091/5.

Eastwest Travel Service Co. Ltd., Room 802, Koreana Hotel, 61-1, 1-ga, T'aep'yongno, Chung-gu. Tel: 735-8734/8.

Global Tours Ltd., 57-9 Sosomun-dong, Hung-gu. Tel: 777-9921/9.

Hannam Tourist Corp., 89-4, Kyong-un-dong, Chongno-gu. Tel: 313-2131.

Kolon Express Tour Co., 12th floor, Sangyong Building, 24-1, 2-ga, Cho-dong, Chung-gu. Tel: 273-5461/5.

Korea Tourist Bureau Ltd., 728 Soch'o-dong, Kangnam-gu. Tel: 585-1191.

Korea Travel Company Ltd., Room 301, Dongyang Building., 112-6, Sogong-dong, Chung-gu. Tel: 777-0981/5.

Lotte Travel Service Ltd., 27-1, Sup'yo-dong, Chung-gu. Tel: 65-4151/5.

Sam Yong Travel Service Co.Ltd., Room 1003, Songgi Building. Tel: 719-4814/7.

Seoul Orient Express Corp., 5th floor, Kyongwun Building, 70 Kyingun-dong, Chongno-gu. Tel: 732-2628/9.

The Korea Express Travel Service Co. Ltd, 58-12, Sosomun-dong, Chung-gu. Tel: 777-8871/6.

The Korea Times Travel Ltd., 12th floor, Korea Times Building, 14 Chunghak-dong, Chongno-gu. Tel: 734-0071.

ORGANIZED TOURS

Guided tours are operated by two of the agents listed above, Global Tours and Korea Tourist Bureau. These range from morning and afternoon tours of Seoul's palaces and markets to two night/three day tours of Kyongju and Pusan. The only way to see P'anmunjom is on a tour such as this. Contact the agencies for further details. Similar tours are run by some other agencies.

EMBASSIES

Argentina: 793-4062
Australia: 720-6490/5
Austria: 723-7330
Belgium: 793-9611
Bolivia: 742-7170
Brazil: 720-4769
Canada: 776-4062/8
Chile: 792-9519
Republic of China: (Taiwan): 776-2721/5
Colombia: 794-5770
Costa Rica: 725-5877
Denmark: 792-4187/9
Dominican Republic: 792-1850
Ecuador: 792-1278
Finland: 732-6223
France: 362-5547/9
Gabon: 562-9912/3
West Germany: 779-3271/3
Guatemala: 793-1319
Haiti: 797-9372
Holy See: 732-5725
India: 724-4278/9

Indonesia: 782-5116/9
Iran: 793-7751/3
Italy: 722-5980
Japan: 733-4272
Liberia: 793-6704
Libya: 532-0306
Malaysia: 792-9203
Mexico: 741-4060
Netherlands: 793-0651/2
New Zealand: 720-4255
Norway: 792-6850
Oman: 797-8846/7
Pakistan: 313-0427/8
Panama: 720-4164
Paraguay: 794-5553
Peru: 792-2235
Philippines: 720-4860
Saudi Arabia: 313-0631/5
Spain: 720-4564
Sweden: 720-4767
Switzerland: 744-9511/4
Thailand: 792-3098
Turkey: 794-0255
United Kingdom: 725-7341/3
United States: 732-2601/19
Uruguay: 798-0561
Venezuela: 741-0036/7

SELECTED KOREAN EMBASSIES ABROAD

Australia (Canberra): tel: 733044
Belgium (Brussels): tel: (02) 375-3980
Canada (Ontario): tel: (613) 232-1715
Republic of China (Taipei): tel: 761-9363
Denmark (Copenhagen): tel: (01) 143123
Finland (Helsinki): tel: 642509
France (Paris): tel: 705-6410
West Germany (Bonn): tel: 0228-218095/6
India (Delhi): tel: 601601/5
Indonesia (Jakarta): tel: 512309
Italy (Rome): tel: 805306
Japan (Tokyo): tel: (03) 452-7611/9
Malaysia (Kuala Lumpur): tel: 482177
Netherlands (The Hague): tel: 070-520621
New Zealand (Wellington): tel: 739073
Norway (Oslo): tel: 562211

Philippines (Metro Manila): tel: 817-827
Portugal (Lisbon): tel: 777176
Singapore: tel: 2561188
Spain (Madrid): 4100053
Sweden (Stockholm): tel: 08/16-04-80
Switzerland (Bern): tel: (031) 431081/2
Thailand (Bangkok): tel: 234-0723/6.
United Kingdom (London): tel: (01) 581-0247/9.
United States (Washington DC): tel: (202) 483-7383.

KOREAN FESTIVALS AND HOLIDAYS

New Year Holiday, January 1-3. Many Koreans, however, still save their best food, wine and clothes for Lunar New Year, which occurs some weeks later.

Independence Movement Day, March 1: marks the March 1, 1919 Independence Movement.

Arbor Day, April 5: tree-planting jamboree.

Buddha's Birthday, 8th day of 4th lunar month, usually early May. See "**Religion**" in "**Culture of Korea**" chapter, above, for a description of the festivities.

Children's Day, May 5: the day for children to be dressed up and taken on excursions.

Memorial Day, June 6: commemorating those who died for their country.

Farmer's Day, June 15: not a national holiday, but observed at farmers' festivals in the countryside with folk dancing and music.

Constitution Day, July 17: patriotic ceremonies in major cities mark the anniversary of the promulgation of the Constitution on July 17, 1948.

Liberation Day, August 15, marking the surrender of Japan to the Allies and Korea's subsequent release from the colonial yoke.

Chusok, 15th day of 8th lunar month, usually mid-September: Korea's ancient harvest thanksgiving festival. After win-ing and dining, families proceed to hill-sides and lake-sides to watch the rising of the harvest moon, the biggest of the year.

Armed Forces Day, October 1: marked by parades and other displays of military pageantry. Major ceremonies are held on the broad plaza on Yoi Island, just south of central Seoul in the Han River.

National Foundation Day, October 3: Also known as Tangun, this holiday commemorates the mythical founding of Korea by Tan-gun in 2333 BC. The ceremonies take place on the summit of Mt. Mani on Kanghwa Island, where the event was supposed to have taken place.

Han'gul Day, October 9: Celebrates the invention of *han'gul*, the Korean alphabet, by King Sejong. Ceremonies at his tomb mark the day.

United Nations Day, October 24: commemorates U.N. soldiers who died defending the south during the Korean War.

Christmas Day. Celebrated throughout the country by Korea's eight million Christians.

Annual festivals

Tongshin-je, 15th day of 1st lunar month; usually around mid-February. An ancient festival related to Lunar New Year festivities and shaman fertility rites; today observed only in remote rural areas.

Unsan Village Ritual, April: A 12-day festival held at a shrine southwest of Unsan Village, Chung- chongnam-do Province, in honor of the local spirit of the mountain. Intangible Cultural Asset No. 9.

Hanshik, 105th day of lunar calendar (March or April): *Hanshik* means "cold food," and in the old days people were not supposed to light fires on this day. Nowadays *hanshik* is an occasion to visit, pay respects to and tidy up the graves of one's ancestors.

Chunhyang Festival, 8th day of 4th lunar month, usually early May: held on the same day as Buddha's Birthday, this festival, at the town of Namwon, Chollapuk Province, celebrates Chunhyang, Korea's favorite heroine, who supposedly lived here. See **Namwon (Off the Beaten Track)** for details of her story. The festival features contests of *pansori*, a form of recitation which originated in the area.

Arang Festival, May 9: Held at Milyang village in Kyongsangnam Province, this festival celebrates the conjugal fidelity of Arang, a popular heroine of the Shilla dynasty. A "Miss Arang Contest" is featured: besides being pretty, the winning girl must demonstrate her skill in literary composition, classical music, calligraphy and embroidery.

Tano (spring) Festival, 5th day of 5th lunar month, (usually in May): Originally an occasion to pray for good harvests, this is a big event in many country towns and villages, with dancing, wrestling matches, swinging contests and shamanistic rituals. Designated Intangible Cultural Asset No. 13, the festival goes on for a whole week in the otherwise somnolent east coast town of Kangnung. In Seoul it is marked with folk dances and shaman ceremonies on the banks of the Han River.

Mahan Folk Festival, October 8: A local festival held in the vicinity of Iksan village in Chollapuk Province, celebrating the history and legends of the Paekche Kingdom. Andong Folk Festival, September 28: Held near the ancient Confucian Academy outside Andong, this festival falls on Confucius's birthday. It features Chajon-nori, "War of Dragons", Intangible Cultural Asset No. 24, in which warriors mounted on monstrous A-frames supported by dozens of burly men strive to throw each other to the ground. Other events include a mask-dance drama and a bridge-crossing game. For more about the archaic town and environs of Andong, see **Off the Beaten Track**.

Shilla Cultural Festival, October

10: One of Korea's brightest, most exuberant festivals. Held in and around Kyongju and celebrating the history and achievements of the Shilla Period, events include classical music at Anapchi Pond, a farmers' folk music contest, archery, wrestling and Buddhist dancing. Flags and lanterns bring the streets of the town to life. One of the must-sees of an autumn trip to Korea. If you plan to stay in the town, make your hotel reservation early.

Paekche Cultural Festival, October 13: Puyo and Kongju's answer to Kyongju's festival, described immediately above. The festival honors the great kings and heroes of Paekche, including the 3,000 palace ladies who hurled themselves to their deaths from Falling Flowers Cliff. See **Off the Beaten Track** for more about this area and its history.

Moyang Castle Festival, ninth day of ninth lunar month, mid-October: Moyang Castle was constructed in 1453, exclusively, it is said, by women, and the festival commemorates the achievement. Thousands of colorfully-dressed women parade along the castle walls. Other activities include singing contests and archery matches.

Halla Cultural Festival, October 18-20: Cheju's annual celebration of its special legacy and identity, the festival begins with the ringing of bells and blowing of whistles throughout the island. Events include art exhibitions and performances of traditional music.

Kaechon (National Foundation) Arts Festival, third day of 10th lunar month (mid-November): held at the town of Chinju, Kyongsangnam-do Province, the festival is famous for its sword- dance, performed by half-a-dozen dancers accompanied by drumming. Contests and exhibitions of calligraphy and landscape painting, poetry, music and traditional drama are among the other events.

MISCELLANEOUS TIPS

TIPPING

Tipping is not the custom in Korea, and just about the only situation where it is

Interior of Seoul National Museum, recently reopened in the Capitol Building after extensive refurbishment.

expected is in the kisaeng house, where quite large tips are left for the ladies responsible for the entertainment. Taxi drivers do not require tipping unless they carry your bag, but it is common practice to let them keep the change when the sum involved is small.

INTRODUCTIONS AND SURNAMES

Korean forms of introduction approximate closely to Japanese ones. The individual introduces himself, bowing slightly and presenting his name card with both hands – giving anything with just one hand is considered impolite.

Korean surnames were borrowed some 2,000 years ago from among China's Old Hundred Names. It seems, however, that only about half a dozen of the Old Hundred appealed to Koreans, for millions of them today share a handful of surnames. Given names therefore assume a disproportionate importance, and when you strike up a friendship with a Korean it is a good idea to commit all his or her names to memory. As in China, surnames always precede given names.

The most common surname in Korea is Kim, which means "gold", followed by Lee ("plum") and Park ("white"). Women retain their maiden names after marriage, so don't be taken aback when Mr Kim introduces you to his wife, Mrs Lee.

GEOGRAPHICAL TERMS

The following terms appear as suffixes after place names in maps, brochures and guides; a familiarity with them will help you to make an intelligent guess about the size of the place being discussed:

-*do:* province
-*si:* major city or large town
-*up:* town
-*kun:* major district
-*myon:* township or village

-*ri:* residential sub-district
-*no, -ro, -'o:* road or street
-*ka:* subsection of road or street
-*gu:* major ward of large city
-*dong:* precinct of a large city, sub-section of a ward.

LOST AND FOUND

If you lose something valuable in Seoul contact the Lost and Found Center, Citizens' Room, Seoul Metropolitan Police Bureau, 24-17-4 Namdaemun-ro, Chung-ku. Tel: 28-9900. You might also tell the Munhwa Broadcasting Co. (tel: 74-6151, 74-2601) and the Tongyang Broadcasting Co. (tel: 23-1211, 28-8211) about it. They may oblige by broadcasting a description of the missing item.

BUSINESS HOURS

Official business hours are 9 am to 6 pm Monday to Friday, 9 am to 1 pm Saturdays. Between November and March clocking-off time is 5 pm. Many private businesses stay open deep into the evening.

Banking hours are 9:30 am to 4:30 pm Monday to Friday, 9:30 am to 1:30 pm on Saturdays.

Most department stores open from 10:30 am to 7:30 pm, with one day off a week. As stores take different days off, you will usually find several open on any day. Sunday trading is universal.

KEEPING CLEAN AND TRIM

A bath-house is *mogyok-tang;* a barber-shop is ibalso. In Korea both are as much a treat as a utility.

The Korean public bath is very similar to the Japanese. Soaping and

Interior of Seoul National Museum, recently reopened in the Capitol Building after extensive refurbishment.

Some baths also have saunas and a corner to take a nap in. They are open for business from early in the morning to around 8 pm.

Besides the basic hair cut, Korean barbers routinely provide manicure, cut-throat shave and scalp massage as well, and sometimes three or four assistants will be busy with a different part of you at once. Other free extras may include ear-cleaning, hot towels, facial creams, pedicures, and complimentary cigarettes and tea - all good reasons for staying in Korea long enough to let your hair grow.

THE ROMANIZATION MESS

Roman orthography in modern Korea might be compared with the situation in Shakespeare's England, where the Bard himself wrote his own name nine different ways. This is because two drastically different systems of romanization are in use, the McCune-Reischauer, which enjoys international recognition, and the Ministry of Education's system, which does not. Faced with these perplexities, most people (including most Koreans, who have little cause to write their own language in Roman letters anyway) tend to improvise according to the way the word sounds to them. This is weird at first, but after a while you may start to enjoy it; there is an odd sense of liberation in being able to spell any way you fancy.

This is how some important place-names come out in the two different systems:
McCune-Reischauer~Ministry of Education
Pusan~Busan   Cheju-do~Jeju-do
Chongno~Jongro Kyongju~Gyeongju
Sorak-san~Solak-san

In common with most English language guides, we have used the Mc-Cune-Reischauer system in this book, with the exception of some names of people where the individuals concerned

have their own preferred Roman form, and the name of the capital, which McCune-Reischauer would spell "Soul".

The only thing to be said for the existence of these two systems is that they do, taken together, help to do justice to the unfamiliarity (to Western ears) and subtlety of Korean pronunciation. Below is a guide to the values of those Korean sounds, as expressed in McCune-Reischauer romanization, which differ substantially from English ones.

l/r: used interchangeably in Korean; no clear distinction made.
a: like *a* in *car*.
ya: like *ya* in *yard*
o: like *u* in *under*.
yo: as in *York*.
u: like *oo* in *boot*, but shorter.
yu: like *you* but shorter.
u: like *u* in *put*.
i: like *ea* in *eat*, but shorter.
ae: like *e* in *wed*.
yae: like *ye* in *yesterday*.
e: like *a* in *aid*.
ye: like *ye* in *yet*.
oe: like *oeu* in French *oeuf* but shorter.
wi: like *wi* in *win*.
ui: like *wi* in *win*, but without lip-rounding.
wa: like *wha* in *whack*.
wo: like *whu* in *whump*.
wae: like *we* in *wear*.
we: like the first vowel sound in *wait*.

INSTANT KOREAN

Numerals:

1 *Il*		2 *Ee*	
3 *Sam*		4 *Sa*	
5 *O*		6 *Yuk*	
7 *Ch'il*		8 *Pal*	
9 *Ku*		10 *Sip*	
11 *Sipee*		20 *Ee-sip*	
30 *Sam-sip*		40 *Sa-sip*	
50 *O-sip*		60 *Yuk-sip*	
70 *Ch'il-sip*		80 *Pal-sip*	
90 *Ku-sip*		100 *Paek*	

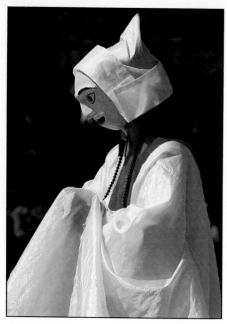

200 *Ee-paek*   300 *Sam-paek*
846 *Pal-paek-sa-sip-yuk*
1,000 *Ch'on*   2,000 *Ee-ch'on*
5,729 *O-ch'on-Ch'il-paek-ee-sip-ku*
10,000 *Man*   20,000 *Ee-man*

Greetings and other civilities

Good morning/afternoon/evening *An-nyong ha-simnikka* or *Annyong haseyo*
Hello (eg. on telephone) *Yobo-seyo*
Yes *Ye*
No *Anio*
Excuse me *Sille-hamnida*
Thank you *Kamsa-hamnida*
You're welcome *Ch'onman-eyo*
Sorry *Mian-hamnida*
See you again *To mannap-sida*
What is your name? *Irumi muo-simnika?*
My name is... *Na-ui irumun...imnida*
Just a moment, please *Cham-kkan man kitari-seyo*
I beg your pardon *Tasi malsumhae chu-seyo*

Phrases and sentence patterns

Where is...? *...odi iss-umnikka?*

ABOVE Masks used in rural festival in Kosong province.

What is that? *Jogosun muo-simnikka?*
That is good *Cho sumnida*
That is bad *Nappumnida*
You are beautiful *Tangsinun yepum-nida*
I like you *Tangsinul joa-hamnida*
Please bring me some... *...chom kata chu-seyo*
Please give me... *...chusip-siyo*
Do you have...? *...iss umnikka?*
How much does it cost? *Olma imnikka?*
It is too expensive *Nomu ppisamnida*
Can you give a discount? *Discountu-rul hal-su-iss- umnikka?*
Can you speak English? *Yong-o hal-su-iss-umnikka?*
How long does it take to get there? *Ol-mana kolimnikka?*
Please stop here *Sewo chu-seyo*
What is this place called? *Yogi-nun odi imnikka?*
Never mind *Kokjong maseyo*

Food and beverages

Korean food *Han chong sik*
beer *Maekchu*
This is delicious *Aju masi sumnida*
Please bring the bill *Kesanso-rul chusip-siyo*
Restaurant *sik-tang*
Bar *sul-jip* Tearoom *Tabang*
For more food and beverage words, see relevant section in **The Culture of Korea**.

Places

Department store *Paekhwa-chom*
Duty-free shop *Myonse-chom*
Local market *Sijang*
Airport *Konghang*
Seoul railway station *Seoul-yok*
Entrance *Ipku*
Exit *Ch'ulku*
Restroom *Hwajang-sil*
Bank *Unhaeng*
Hotel *Hotel*
Good Korean inn *Cho-un yogwan*
Post Office *Uche-kuk*
Police station *Pach'ul-so*
Public telephone *Kongchung-chonwa*

Subway *Chi-hach'ol*
Terminal *Chongjom*
South Gate Market *Namdae-mun sijang*
East Gate Market *Dongdae-mun sijang*
Sejong Cultural Center *Sejong mun-wha-hoekwan*

Sample sentences
Where is the restroom? *Hwajang-sil odi iss umnikka?*
Please bring me some beer? *Maekchu chom kata chu-seyo.*
Do you have coffee? *Kopi iss-umnikka?*

Suggested further reading

There is not an embarrassment of good books in English about Korea (though there are not a few that are quite embarrassing). Here is a brief selection of volumes which are helpful or interesting or both.

A New History of Korea by Ki-baik Lee, Cambridge, Mass., Harvard-Yenching Institute/Harvard University Press, translated by Edward W. Wagner and Edward J. Shultz, 1984. Readable and authoritative single-volume history by top Korean scholar.

Koreana by Peter Hyun, Seoul, Korea Britannica, 1984. A profile of Korea's history and culture, dependable if a little stolid. Heavily illustrated with color photographs.

A Handbook of Korea, ed. Kim Young-kwon, Seoul, Seoul International Publishing House, 6th Edition, 1987. Useful almanac for those who want to know *lots* more.

Korea's Cultural Roots, Dr Jon Carter Covell, Elizabeth, New Jersey/Seoul, Hollym International Corp., 1981. A chatty ramble through the traditional culture by this inexhaustible and gleefully controversial scholar and longterm resident.

Korea's Kyongju, Edward B. Adams, Seoul, Seoul International Publishing House, 1979. Difficult to use as a guide, but indispensable for anybody with a serious interest in Kyongju.

Five Thousand Years of Korean Art, San Francisco, Asian Art Museum of San Francisco, 1979. Catalogue of the famous exhibition, with an enlightening introduction and many marvelous plates.

Fragrance of Spring, Chai Hong Sim, Seoul, Po Chin Chai, 1970. Charmingly ingenuous English version of Korea's favorite love story.

Inside Seoul: The Honam Oil Guide to Seoul, Seoul, Benedict Press, 1985. Highly detailed, very practical guide to Seoul, aimed particularly at resident foreigners, with dozens of brilliant maps. Information on everything from jogging to pizza, from taxidermists to plastic flowers.

Korea and Taiwan: A Travel Survival Kit, Geoff Crowther, South Yarra, Lonely Planet Publications, 1982. Practical though far from comprehensive budget guide to the country. Good on the nitty-gritty (cheap restaurants, bars, inns) like all Lonely Planet titles.

Index

1988 SEOUL OLYMPIAD (September 17 to October 2 1988)

SPORT \ DATE Sept	17 Sat	18 Sun	19 Mon	20 Tue	21 Wed	22 Thu	23 Fri	24 Sat	25 Sun	26 Mon	27 Tue	28 Wed	29 Thu	30 Fri	1 Sat	2 Sun
Opening ceremony	•															
Archery											•	•	•	•		
Athletics							•	•	•	•		•	•	•	•	•
Basketball	•	•	•	•	•	•	•	•	•	•	•	•	•	•		
Boxing		•	•	•	•	•	•	•	•	•	•	•	•		•	•
Canoeing										•	•	•	•	•	•	
Cycling		•		•	•	•	•	•	•	•						
Equestrian sports			•	•	•	•	•	•	•	•	•		•	•		•
Fencing			•	•	•	•	•		•	•	•	•	•			
Football	•	•	•	•	•	•		•	•		•			•	•	
Gymnastics		•	•	•	•	•	•	•	•		•	•	•			
Handball				•		•	•	•	•	•	•	•	•	•	•	
Hockey		•		•	•	•	•	•	•	•	•	•	•	•	•	
Judo								•	•	•	•	•	•	•	•	
Modern Pentathlon		•	•	•	•											
Rowing		•	•	•	•	•	•	•								
Shooting		•	•	•	•	•	•	•								
Swimming		•	•	•	•	•	•	•	•							
Diving									•	•	•	•	•	•	•	•
Synchronized swimming									•	•	•		•		•	
Water polo			•	•	•		•	•		•	•					
Table tennis			•	•	•	•	•	•	•							
Tennis				•	•	•	•	•	•	•	•	•	•		•	
Volleyball		•		•	•	•	•	•	•	•	•	•	•	•	•	•
Weightlifting			•	•	•	•	•		•	•	•	•	•			
Wrestling			•	•	•	•	•		•	•	•	•	•			
Yachting			•	•	•	•			•	•	•					
Closing Ceremony																•

DS 982.4 .P674 1988 c.1
Popham, Peter.
The insider's guide to Kore

DATE DUE	
OCT 2 5 1999	

GAYLORD   PRINTED IN U.S.A.